Panic at the Bank

How John Rusnak lost AIB $691,000,000

ONE WEEK LOAN

Also by Conor O'Clery
  Phrases Make History Here (1986)
  Melting Snow (1991)
  America, A Place Called Hope? (1992)
  The Greening of the White House (1996)
  Ireland in Quotes, A History of the 20th Century (1999)

Panic at the Bank

How John Rusnak lost AIB $691,000,000

Siobhán Creaton and Conor O'Clery

Gill & Macmillan

Gill & Macmillan Ltd
Hume Avenue, Park West, Dublin 12
with associated companies throughout the world
www.gillmacmillan.ie
© Siobhán Creaton and Conor O'Clery 2002
0 7171 3563 2
Index compiled by Cover To Cover
Design and print origination by Carole Lynch
Printed by the Woodprintcraft Group Ltd, Dublin

This book is typeset in Goudy 10.5 on 13.5 pt.

*The paper used in this book comes from the wood pulp of
managed forests. For every tree felled, at least one tree
is planted, thereby renewing natural resources.*

A CIP catalogue record for this book is available
from the British Library.

5

Contents

Preface

This book reconstructs the dramatic events which caused Ireland's biggest bank to fall victim to the world's fourth-largest currency trading scandal. It tells the story of how John Rusnak, a foreign exchange trader at AIB subsidiary Allfirst's small treasury unit in Baltimore, Maryland, lost $691 million of the bank's money on the world's currency markets.

Rusnak's foreign exchange bets were so big he moved markets. New York banks vied for his business. He was fêted with trips to Las Vegas and the Super Bowl. For five years he lost money. But no one did anything to stop him getting his hands on hundreds of millions of dollars to gamble his way out of trouble, only to lose it all.

Panic at the Bank explains how he got away with it for so long, as top executives at both banks ignored or dismissed signs that something was badly wrong. It is also the story of how AIB's bold venture into American regional banking was bedevilled by a clash of cultures, with a former bank clerk from Cork going head to head with an elite 'blue-blood' banker in a boardroom struggle for power high above Baltimore's inner harbour.

It is the story of a breakdown of morale and staff turmoil at Maryland's second-largest bank, which contributed to a spectacular collapse in controls and a series of management lapses that allowed a rogue trader's losses to go undetected for years.

This account is reconstructed from many hours of interviews with people involved in both banks and others central to the story. To them we offer our sincere thanks while respecting their desire to remain anonymous. We have also drawn on our own knowledge of events from reporting the story for the *Irish Times* as it occurred, and on extensive documentation, including the Ludwig Report into the fraudulent trading which provided a road map through the deceptions created by John Rusnak, as well as court papers, regulatory filings, bank reports, internal memos and newspaper archives.

Finally, we would like to thank all those who gave us advice, help, guidance and insights into the world of banking and currency trading, and who helped in any way in the compilation and production of this book, especially David O'Sullivan, Vincent Boland, Paul O'Neill and Paul Teetley.

Chronology

1983:   Allied Irish Banks announced that it was to take a majority shareholding in First Maryland Bank, the second-biggest bank in Baltimore, for $95 million.

1989:   AIB takes control of First Maryland for a total investment of $150 million. Later that year it bought the tiny Columbia National Bank in Washington.

1991:   First Maryland purchased York Bank for $129 million cash.

1997:   First Maryland purchased the Harrisburg, Pennsylvania-based Dauphin Deposit for $1.36 billion in cash and stock, making it one of the top 50 US banks.

1997-1999: First Maryland sold its credit card business, Omni Corp, which had been established in 1982.

1999:   First Maryland changed its name to Allfirst.

2002:   In February Allfirst announced that a currency trader, John Rusnak, had defrauded the bank of $750 million. This figure was later reduced to $691.2 million.

2002:   In September AIB's board of directors considered merging Allfirst with a larger American bank while retaining a 25 per cent minority stake in the Baltimore bank.

1

Gobsmacked

On the morning of Sunday 3 February 2002 a number of cars drove together through the near-deserted streets of downtown Baltimore. They converged on South Charles Street, and turned into the underground car park of the twenty-five-storey office block that was home to Allfirst Bank. The occupants got out and took the elevator to the twelfth floor. There they waited, glancing impatiently at their watches. At precisely midday, one of them lifted a telephone and punched in a number. The others watched as he spoke into the receiver. When he was finished talking he put it down sharply.

'He says to call back at nine.'

Someone uttered an expletive.

The person at the other end of the line, however, had no intention of taking any call at nine. For John Rusnak that brief exchange was his last contact with the bank where he had worked for eight years. He had stalled them for the last time and he knew he couldn't do it again. The men gathered in the bank's trading room, colleagues with whom he worked, drank and played golf, were going through his trades. They would soon realise that he had deceived them and made fools of them almost every day, for five years.

They had been so easy to mislead for so long, but John Rusnak's luck had run out the previous week. On Thursday a manager demanded to see confirmations of twelve foreign currency trades he had supposedly made with Asian banks. A clerk had telephoned the banks and they had denied all knowledge of them. Rusnak then printed off a dozen fake confirmations and left them in the back office on Friday morning. No other bank in the world would accept confirmations from a trader, but the ploy had worked before and Rusnak hoped against hope that it would work again.

But this time the manager thought they looked bogus. He called a meeting with Rusnak and his supervisor, Bob Ray. He said that he needed immediate confirmations by telephone.

Rusnak reacted as he usually did when faced with disclosure: he threw a tantrum. He stormed out of the office and threatened to quit if they didn't stop questioning everything he did. After ten minutes Rusnak came back and apologised. He told them he would supply the telephone number of the broker who handled the trades. He had it at home and they should call him at midday on Sunday when the markets opened in Asia. They could verify the trades through the broker, he said.

There was no broker of course, but they still wanted to believe him. No one tried to stop him gathering his personal belongings from his desk, putting them in a box and taking the elevator to ground level. He walked out of the building for the last time as Allfirst's star foreign currency trader. Rusnak knew that when he didn't return, they would start double-checking all his trades. In his desktop PC they would find a file named 'Fake Docs' where he stored fraudulent trade confirmations. It would not take them long to realise that he had lost hundreds of millions of dollars on the foreign exchange currency markets when they had believed he was making money for the bank all those years.

Rusnak now had to figure out what to do. He needed time to think. He put his wife, Linda, and their two children into the family's red Chevy Tahoe, drove down the driveway from their suburban Mount Washington home into Smith Avenue, and headed towards the beltway and out of town.

The small group of executives stayed at Allfirst Bank head-quarters all that Sunday afternoon and into the evening. At nine, Larry Smith, the executive who had called Rusnak earlier, punched in his number again. The phone rang unanswered in the empty house. Smith kept trying. He didn't give up until well after midnight.

Next day, Monday 4 February 2002, Rusnak did not turn up for work and the crisis broke. Thoroughly alarmed, David Cronin, the head of the bank's forty-strong treasury unit, and Bob Ray, Rusnak's direct supervisor, drove out to Rusnak's house. If what they feared was true, their careers and reputations lay in ruins.

Cronin had been a fixture at the Baltimore bank since it was bought outright by Allied Irish Banks in 1989 and he had been sent by Dublin to run the treasury department and liaise with the American management. He and Bob Ray had hired Rusnak eight years earlier to make extra revenue through betting on the foreign exchange markets. Ray for his part regarded Rusnak as his protégé, someone special who had unique skills in the complicated business of making money through buying and selling options. He protected him every time a row blew up at the bank over his trades, which had been happening frequently in the last few months. Only on Friday he had warned the treasury staff, after Rusnak had stormed out of the room, that if the bank's foreign currency wizard did quit because of their tight scrutiny, some of them would lose their jobs.

Cronin and Ray turned off Interstate 83 towards Smith Avenue, the long, tree-shaded road of upper-middle-class homes where Rusnak lived. It was familiar territory to Cronin. His own home was only a mile away and he knew well where Rusnak's house was located. Cronin and Rusnak were both active parishioners at the Shrine of the Sacred Heart Catholic Church on Smith Avenue. In the little suburban parish they were both highly regarded as important executives at Allfirst.

The Irish-owned bank was the second-largest bank in Maryland, and its blue logo with white and orange squares adorned more than 250 branches and 575 automated teller machines in Maryland, Pennsylvania, Delaware, north Virginia and Washington DC. It was an important part of everyday life in Baltimore, where 2,000 of its 6,000 employees lived. Allfirst posters in bank windows told potential customers: 'You focus on what's really important, we'll focus on helping you get it.' The name spelled out in neon on top of its twenty-two-storey corporate headquarters by the harbour was clearly visible for miles around. It wasn't the sort of bank where one would expect to find a solitary foreign exchange dealer moving worldwide markets with huge bets.

The two treasury bosses drove to the sloping tarmacadam avenue that led up to Rusnak's front door, past the side windows with green shutters through which antique vases could be glimpsed. A couple of wooden sledges and fold-out chrome scooters were propped up near a multi-coloured plastic playhouse. They pulled up outside the door. No one answered. There was no sign of movement inside.

The two men drove back to the bank. They had a bunch of what were almost certainly bogus confirmations of trades worth hundreds of millions of dollars. They had a missing trader. But they could not

yet bring themselves to tell the chief executive of Allfirst, Susan
Keating, what was going to hit her. Not until 3.30 in the afternoon
did Cronin take the lift to the executive suite on the twenty-second
floor to break the news. He had, he said, an emergency situation.

It was not an easy meeting. Keating, stunned, called the Allfirst
chairman, Frank Bramble. She got him on his car telephone. Since
being made bank chairman in 1999, Bramble had spent a lot of time
away from his office, attending civic functions or flying back and
forth across the Atlantic to board meetings in Dublin. 'I think we
have a serious situation,' Keating said.

Bramble sped back to the bank where Cronin briefed him on
Rusnak's disappearance. They were still going through Rusnak's
trades, the treasurer said, and as yet did not know what the bank was
facing, but it was certain that they had a major financial scandal on
their hands. It wasn't just the money. All their jobs were on the line.

An hour after her meeting with Cronin, Susan Keating dialled
the number in Dublin of AIB chief executive, Michael Buckley. It
was 9.30 pm in Ireland. Buckley, in the top post at Ireland's biggest
bank for only nine months, had been celebrating his 57th birthday
that day. He had every reason to be in good spirits. AIB was
performing well. In two weeks' time he was scheduled to announce
record annual profits of more than €1 billion for the company.
Buckley was having a cup of tea and watching television with his
wife, Anne, at home in Rathmines, after hosting a dinner for senior
management, when the telephone rang.

Buckley would say later that the degree of shock on taking that
call from Keating was on the same scale as hearing that there was a
bereavement in the family. 'It was a bit like hearing my brother had
died in a car accident,' he said. 'I never thought it could happen in
our bank. I have a reasonable understanding of risk management, and
my belief was that our risk management processes were very strong.'

Buckley telephoned Gary Kennedy, the AIB group financial officer,
who was putting his ten-year-old daughter to bed. 'I've just got a
phone call with some very bad news from the United States,' he said.

Before the evening was out, Buckley ordered a small group of
executives to meet in the bank first thing in the morning to decide
what should be done and in the meantime to say absolutely nothing.
He couldn't call the AIB chairman, Lochlann Quinn, just yet; Quinn

was on an Aer Lingus flight to Dublin from New York, where he had delivered a lecture to business leaders at the World Economic Forum on the need for more stringent financial controls in corporations in the wake of the collapse of the Texas energy trading company, Enron.

It was still dark when Buckley and members of his crisis group drove into the grounds of AIB's modern low-rise headquarters in Ballsbridge, south of Dublin city centre. Buckley called Lochlann Quinn, now back in Dublin, to tell him the news. The AIB chief executive and his group decided on several emergency measures. He instructed AIB group treasurer, Pat Ryan, to select a small team from the treasury and get to Dublin airport to catch the first available flight to the United States. AIB needed to know from its own people how much money was missing, whether it was the work of a single rogue trader, and whether any other bank employees were involved. The most urgent priority was to calculate the total losses so they could assess the damage and notify the Stock Exchange. In the meantime he ordered the suspension of Cronin and Ray, two other officials in direct management line above the trader, and two more staff members who were involved in supervising Rusnak.

The crisis meetings went on all day without the other staff at AIB headquarters knowing what was happening. Until late on Tuesday only a small core group of officials in AIB was aware that a financial scandal of global proportions was about to hit the bank. They included Buckley, Kennedy, Colm Doherty, who was head of AIB's Capital Markets division, Eugene Sheehy, who ran the bank's operations in Ireland, and Catherine Burke, head of corporate communications.

In Baltimore on Tuesday morning, the bank's lawyer contacted the city office of the Federal Bureau of Investigation. A trader had caused massive losses and they did not know where he was, the lawyer said. FBI officials Steven Graybill and Kevin Comiskey drove to Rusnak's house in Mount Washington to look for him.

Because of the five-hour time difference between Dublin and Baltimore, Ryan and his group were able to get to Baltimore and take over the investigation well before the end of Tuesday. Alongside Allfirst finance officials they worked through the night checking the trades Rusnak had made with Asian banks. It was very late in Dublin when Pat Ryan came through on the phone to give Buckley his best estimate of the extent of the losses that Rusnak had run up without anyone noticing. The good news was that it would not break the bank. The bad news was that it was calculated at $750 million. It was the biggest bank fraud since Nick Leeson brought down Barings Investment Bank in 1995 with losses of £850 million, the equivalent of $1.4 billion. Anything affecting AIB would have a significant impact on Ireland. It was the largest company on the Irish Stock Exchange, employing 31,000 people.

Buckley worked with Catherine Burke and Jim Milton, a senior partner with the Dublin PR firm, Murray Consultants, and a regular spin doctor for the bank, on a strategy for damage limitation. They decided to release the news in two stages. They would issue a statement first thing in the morning frankly admitting the extent of the losses, but emphasising all the steps AIB had taken to investigate suspected fraud and deal with those responsible. Then Buckley would go on radio to reassure customers that it would not break the bank.

A call was put through late in the evening to the editor of 'Morning Ireland', the 7.30 am news programme on Ireland's national radio station, Radio Telefís Éireann, to say that Buckley would be available in the morning to talk about a breaking news story. Intrigued, RTÉ's business reporter, Geraldine Harney, arrived at the RTÉ studios in the suburb of Donnybrook at 5.00 am to find out what the story was. At 7.15 am a statement was faxed to the studio, announcing that AIB was investigating losses of $750 million at its American subsidiary, and that the losses had been incurred over a year because of the actions of one trader. Five minutes later Buckley arrived at the studio with Catherine Burke. The presenter put Buckley on air immediately after the news was announced.

AIB was the victim of a determined fraud by one trader, the AIB chief executive said. It was a heavy blow to the bank. But it was not like the Nick Leeson affair which brought down Barings Bank. AIB would still make a profit after tax of €400 million, about $375 million. It would be business as usual for customers and staff.

The presenter, Cathal MacCoille, invited Geraldine Harney to comment. 'Well, my first reaction is that I am gobsmacked!' she said, using a colloquialism that probably summed up the feelings of early-morning commuters listening-in on car radios. 'You think you have heard it all and then you get a story like this.'

Harney then rattled off a series of scathing questions: 'Are you alarmed that his bosses didn't know what was going on? ... You would have thought that after what happened at Barings and to Nick Leeson that financial institutions would put in place regulations to ensure that one person could not do this again. He had at least four superiors and as far as you know none of them knew?... Surely it does a lot of damage to your reputation... what with all the great management you have within the bank that has enabled you over all of the years to make so much money?'

'We have a very complex and adequate series of checks and balances in the same way that if you have a house and you have a very good alarm system you have a lot of confidence about that,' replied Buckley. 'This has been a blow but AIB is still very strongly capitalised.' The 'fine people in AIB' would repair the damage.

Michael Buckley repeated his points at an analysts' conference call and a press conference in bank headquarters. 'Where is Rusnak?' a reporter asked. 'He legged it,' replied Buckley.

AIB chairman, Lochlann Quinn, told the *Irish Times* that there was 'considerable evidence of collusion in the fraud.' Bogus fax numbers on the counterfeit confirmations suggested that, he said.

The implication for AIB's American subsidiary was that if there was no collusion then management controls had completely failed, with consequences for jobs up the line, perhaps to the very top. Banks where shareholders' money is wagered on foreign currency movements are supposed to maintain tight controls to prevent a lone trader succumbing to temptation by hiding his losses or embezzling money for himself or a partner.

Bank officials who monitor a trader's activities in the front office are deliberately kept apart in what is known as a back office, usually on a separate floor. The back office must enter all transactions in the bank's computer system for verification with counterparties. In AIB's foreign currency operation in Dublin, the back office verifies every trade electronically within minutes. If Rusnak was acting alone at Allfirst, then it meant that he was verifying his own trades and if that were so, there was a collapse of controls and accountability would go right up to the top, not just in Baltimore but in Dublin. If he did not have other employees helping him then it was 'collective stupidity or a ship of fools,' commented David Gilmore, a partner at Foreign

Exchange Analytics in the *New York Times*.

Meanwhile Allfirst officials informed local and federal bank regulators of the losses, and bank examiners from the Federal Reserve Bank in Richmond, Virginia, and from Maryland's Commission of Financial Regulation began to arrive at bank headquarters in South Charles Street. They had an overriding concern: to establish if Maryland's second-largest bank, one of the top fifty banks in the United States, was on the point of collapse.

Officials at Allfirst were in a state of shock. 'We could not get our heads around how big it was,' said Maurice Crowley, the chief finance officer. Allfirst executives called a press conference at bank headquarters at midday. For once the hackneyed term 'ashen-faced' was appropriate to describe how Bramble and Keating looked as they entered the bank's conference room where dozens of American, British and Irish journalists were crowded around a massive oval table. 'This room's usually too big,' said Bramble in an attempt at humour, looking at the crush of bodies. Bramble, Keating and Pat Ryan stood together by a podium near the door. There was no microphone.

Ryan, with his soft Irish accent, had difficulty making himself understood, especially to the American reporters. It was a painful moment for the 56-year-old Co Clare man. He had announced in January that he intended taking early retirement after a distinguished career as the 'father figure of the Irish money markets'. As head of risks, audit and compliance in the AIB group he was technically responsible for Allfirst's treasury. But AIB had for years allowed its American subsidiary to run itself. The 'light hand' approach meant that the treasury in Baltimore was the only place in the Irish bank's international network of trading offices which had its own internal audit team and was not audited by AIB itself. Cronin reported directly to Susan Keating and not to him. Ryan's duty was only to allocate risk limits to Allfirst. It was painful, too, on a personal level. He knew Cronin well, having worked with him as a foreign exchange dealer in the Central Bank of Ireland two decades earlier, and they had kept in close contact over the years.

'Obviously we are shocked by the amount of this loss,' said Bramble. The bank has a 'very small foreign exchange trading function,' he said. 'It appears to have been a very sophisticated, well thought-out fraud, very cleverly done, over a period of time. He found a way to crack our internal control systems. AIB and Allfirst have had very strong internal control systems.' He added that 'it appears the fraud was perpetrated over time with this trader operating within his limits.' Suspicions had been raised when David Cronin had asked Rusnak to lower the bank's exposures in January and had 'developed some level of push-back from this individual.' He apparently could not bear to cite Rusnak by name.

'It is very upsetting also because we have had a year when the core business here has been very profitable,' said Keating, who had been under pressure from Dublin to improve the bank's performance. The fraud had occurred in the section of the bank with which she was least familiar. She expressed bewilderment at Rusnak's disappearance. 'Until Monday he was an employee of good standing, he performed well over the years, he was a solid performer, [and] he was considered an upstanding member of the community.' She added: 'We had controls in place to review risk. It was extremely disappointing to all of us that there was a breakdown in the whole control system.' Asked if Rusnak was allowed to trade at home she said he was not.

Ryan offered an explanation for the behaviour of a rogue trader. 'Some do it for profit,' he said. 'Some do it because it's a pride issue. They start with small mistakes which they have covered up in some way and the thing snowballs. Often it isn't direct personal gain.' He said that some 'red flags' had raised suspicions when the annual management review of the treasury operation began early in January. When told he was over-exposed, Rusnak had replied that if he was forced to reduce his exposure he couldn't trade. Ryan was also insistent that it was not like the Nick Leeson case. 'In no way is it like that. He brought down a bank,' he said.

But it *was* looking like the Nick Leeson story all over again.

The English trader had operated without proper controls in Singapore, far away from head office, intimidating anyone who questioned what he was doing. The Bank of England had drawn three conclusions from the Barings Bank collapse: The losses were incurred by reason of unauthorised and concealed trading activities; the true position was not noticed earlier by reason of a serious failure of controls and managerial confusion; and the external auditors, supervisors or regulators had not detected the true position prior to the collapse.

Allfirst would now have to face an inquiry to ascertain how it had succumbed to a trader with an audacity to match that of Nick Leeson, and whether the conclusions of the Bank of England about Singapore also applied in Baltimore. Contacted by journalists in London, Leeson had one message for Rusnak: 'Give yourself up.'

In Dublin, Buckley and his group had acted quickly to contain the crisis, but investors were pulling out of AIB stocks. With the bank standing to lose about 60 per cent of its profits for 2001, the company's shares fell by 17 per cent on the Dublin market. AIB was suddenly vulnerable to a takeover. Almost 52 million AIB shares were bought and sold and more than €2 billion was wiped off the bank's stock market value for a time. On Wall Street, Allied Irish Banks American Depositary Receipts fell $3.78, closing at $19.77, and on the London Stock Exchange, AIB's share price fell 15 per cent to £11.30.

The Irish Taoiseach (Prime Minister), Bertie Ahern, took the unusual step of speaking in the Dáil, Ireland's parliament, to allay fears that the country's biggest bank was on the point of collapse or of being bought by a foreign financial institution. 'There is no danger to AIB account holders of any loss of funds or indeed the sovereignty of the bank,' Ahern said.

In Dublin, Lochlann Quinn called an emergency meeting of directors for the following day. The meeting, said Quinn, would be 'to establish the complexity of what is involved and why the systems did not work and whether some people didn't do their jobs.'

2

Appalling Vista

As the directors of Allied Irish Banks made their way into the boardroom of the bank's Ballsbridge headquarters for a crisis meeting on the afternoon of Thursday 7 February, they filed past a painting that might have reflected their mood over the loss of hundreds of millions of dollars: Hughie O'Donnell's 'On Our Knees'.

With the Rusnak scandal threatening to bring Ireland's largest bank to its knees, Quinn had sent out confidential emergency calls to the twelve other board members on Tuesday morning, asking them to assemble for an emergency board meeting two days later to consider what to do about this 'blow to the bank and a blow to the credibility of the bank.'

Assembling around the circular mahogany boardroom table that afternoon were some of the wealthiest and most influential people in Ireland.

Lochlann Quinn himself, 60, urbane and intensely private, began his career as the head of Arthur Andersen's audit department in Dublin. He accumulated considerable wealth through his twenty-six per cent share in Glen Dimplex, a private company he helped found that had grown from a small enterprise in Newry into one of the world's largest suppliers of electrical appliances, with brand names like Morphy Richards, Dimplex and Belling. AIB had endeavoured to make the chairman feel at home. His black-leather upholstered office in AIB was adorned with Louis Le Brocquy's 'Cuchulainn VI' tapestry, Jack B Yeats' 'Now or Never', and several sculptures selected from AIB's one-thousand-piece Irish art collection. Quinn along with Martin Naughton, chairman of Glen Dimplex, had a fifty per cent holding in Landmark Investments, owner of the five star Merrion Hotel in Dublin, one of the world's top fifty hotels, where the lobby was also a showcase for Irish art. He was one of Ireland's new generation of philanthropists: in 2001 he paid €2.6 million for

Le Brocquy's 'A Family' which had hung in the Milan offices of Nestlé, and donated it to the National Gallery of Ireland so that it would stay in the country, and he gave €5 million to the Quinn School of Business undergraduate faculty in the Michael Smurfit Graduate School of Business in Dublin. His passions ranged from golf to sports cars, including a green Ferrari, and especially to fine wines. Quinn owned a €34 million Bordeaux vineyard, Château de Fieuzal, which produced around ten thousand cases of Pessac-Léognan, Grand Cru Classé Graves red wine each year. Ever with an eye on business, he suggested to former AIB chairman, Tom Mulcahy, now chairman of Aer Lingus, Ireland's national airline, in a note referring to the Rusnak crisis that 'despite current difficulties, life goes on', that the selection of wines on premier class on Aer Lingus might be expanded. The cash-strapped airline replied that it found his Château de Fieuzal a little too expensive.

Deputy AIB chairman, John McGuckian, 62, was the longest serving AIB director and a prominent Northern Ireland Catholic businessman. Like Quinn, he had also amassed a considerable fortune and developed a taste for fine art. McGuckian was chairman of AIB's banking operations in Northern Ireland, First Trust, and chairman of Ulster Television. He had witnessed all the high and low points of the bank's fortunes over twenty-five years.

Michael Buckley, 57, was AIB's chief executive and a former managing director of the group's Poland Division and capital markets, a role that gave him some insight into the world of currency trading.

The other directors included Adrian Burke, 60, a former managing partner of Arthur Andersen and deputy president of the Institute of Chartered Accountants in Ireland, and a long-time associate of Quinn's. He had a key role on the board as chairman of its four-member audit committee, which met five or six times a year to review the bank's own audit practices and monitor the work of its external auditors, PricewaterhouseCoopers, and to assess the effectiveness of AIB's internal controls to prevent fraud.

Padraic Fallon, 55, knew something about the money markets. He was the chairman and former editor of *Euromoney Institutional Investor*, the bible of international money and stock markets. Like McGuckian he had sat through several crisis meetings as a member of the board since 1988, and like Quinn and McGuckian he was also known as a wealthy connoisseur of art.

Dermot Gleeson, 53, from AIB's heartland of Cork, was the board's legal expert. He was a former Fine Gael attorney general and was a high-profile barrister with a court room reputation for tough questioning and mastery of complex detail. He, too, was a wine connoisseur and also had an interest in a five star hotel, the Four Seasons, conveniently located across the road from AIB's headquarters.

There was only one woman board member. Carol Moffett, 49, like most of her co-directors, belonged to Ireland's wealthy elite. When she was just 19 she had taken over her father's small Moffett Engineering firm in Co Monaghan and netted £11 million when it was sold in 1997. She spent much of her time in Portugal where she had a home at the Quinta de Lago resort owned by another super-rich Irish citizen, Esat Telecom founder, Denis O'Brien.

The other directors were: Don Godson, 62, a former chief executive of the Irish buildings materials group CRH; Derek Higgs, 58, deputy chairman of British Land plc, independently wealthy and who would later come to prominence when the UK's Chancellor of the Exchequer, Gordon Brown, asked him to review the role of non-executive directors in Britain in the wake of the Enron scandal in the US, including the responsibilities of audit committee members; Gary Kennedy, 43, AIB's group director for finance, risk and enterprise networks and e-business, and a former managing director of Northern Telecom; Jim O'Leary, 45, former chief economist at Bank of Ireland-owned Davy Stockbrokers and now a lecturer and commentator on economics; and Michael J Sullivan, 62, a former US ambassador to Ireland and former governor of Wyoming who brought some American banking experience to the board as a one-time director of Wyoming National-West Bank. Like so many AIB people he had family roots in Cork.

Frank Bramble, the Allfirst chairman, was also a member of the AIB board and took part in the board meeting through a trans-Atlantic video link-up.

Most of the directors had sat through several crisis meetings in the same boardroom, the most acute having taken place less than three years earlier. That was when AIB had been forced to pay IR£90 million in a settlement with the Irish Revenue Commissioners over non-compliance with a tax on bank deposits known as the Deposit

Interest Retention Tax, or DIRT tax. It was the largest tax settlement in the history of the state. AIB's former Group Internal Auditor, Tony Spollen, had retired some years previously after challenging what he alleged was a bank policy of non-compliance with the DIRT tax, only to be vindicated when a government commission of inquiry heard evidence that AIB bank managers had encouraged clients to evade the tax on their deposit accounts by using overseas addresses, sometimes even supplied by a bank official. Dermot Gleeson had represented AIB at the DIRT inquiry in 1999 and was invited by Quinn to join the board a year later. The episode had severely damaged AIB's reputation as a law-abiding pillar of Irish society. One disgruntled shareholder, Niall Murphy, had kept the controversy going through a web site, AIBDIRT.com.

The board meeting lasted four hours. There was incredulity about the extent of the losses, which in the early hours of the investigation AIB had hoped would only be in the tens of millions. The precise sum was now being calculated at 'ground zero', as the twelfth floor of Allfirst's headquarters quickly became known: Rusnak had gambled away $691.2 million, slightly less than the $750 million that Pat Ryan's team had estimated on Tuesday. But they were now uncovering evidence at Allfirst that the fraud went back five years, not just one, opening up an appalling vista of long-term dereliction of duty. Directors had to face the fact that controls at the treasury in AIB's American subsidiary had collapsed, and the possibility that there had been collusion within the bank of some kind, and possibly with traders at other financial institutions outside Allfirst.

What made it worse was the fact that Allfirst was supposed to be the jewel in AIB's crown, the American acquisition held up by investors and fund managers alike as a model for other European banks looking to expand.

It was not an easy four hours for Bramble, who said he had been planning to retire in the near future, partly because of the strain of commuting across the Atlantic to board meetings once every month. He had left his retirement just a little too late.

The directors agreed to announce to the media its 'extreme disquiet that controls and supervision of the treasury operations at Allfirst had failed to uncover at a far earlier stage the fraudulent activities.' They decided on a measure of last resort to restore investor confidence: the appointment of an outsider, an 'eminent person with standing and expertise in the financial services industry', to probe what went wrong. This would mean turning over all records and documents to investigators and publishing what could be extremely painful findings.

All the board members around the table were aware that the stakes were high. None of them knew just what the investigators would find when they started turning over stones.

The eminent person chosen by the board was Eugene A Ludwig of the Promontory Financial Group of Washington DC. Coincidentally he came from York, Pennsylvania, where Allfirst owned a small subsidiary known as York Bank. But for a few hanging chads in the Florida recount after the 2000 US presidential election, Ludwig might have been Treasury Secretary in a Gore administration. The 54-year-old banker was regarded as one of America's top financial regulators and with his pro-Democratic credentials had been widely tipped for a top job if Vice-President Al Gore had become president.

Ludwig had made his reputation as US Comptroller of the Currency from 1993 to 1998, a post to which he was appointed by his friend, Bill Clinton, a former classmate at Yale Law School and fellow Rhodes scholar at Oxford. At a cabinet meeting after his appointment Ludwig proposed to the President some radical reforms for what had been a little-known office attached to the US Treasury. 'Is this the right thing to do?' asked Clinton. 'Yes it is,' Ludwig said. Clinton just looked across the cabinet table and said, 'Then just go do it', according to Ludwig's own account.

Over the following five years Ludwig made the office one of the most powerful regulatory forces in the federal government. As chief supervisor and regulator for the 3,000 national banks in the US, he presided over one of the most revolutionary periods in American banking history. He liberalised banking laws to stop the defection of corporate clients to other institutions with better access to bond and equity markets. Under his guidance banks were empowered to offer services in securities and insurance previously forbidden under a 1934 Act. He pushed for risk-prediction models and tighter supervision of trading in volatile investments like derivatives and options – one of the instruments used by Rusnak at Allfirst in his foreign currency dealings. The insurance industry hated Ludwig's pro-bank reforms. 'I was quite pilloried at the time by the interest groups as a wild man or something,' he recalled.

Ludwig's background was not without some controversy. He took part in a White House coffee morning organised by the Democratic National Committee in May 1996 to give top bankers access to President Clinton, later acknowledging he made a mistake but ignoring calls to resign. The *Washington Post* took him to task again in 1999 for helping to raise money for Al Gore's presidential campaign.

When his term as Comptroller of the Currency ended in 1998, Ludwig declined an offer to serve a second spell. He joined the Promontory Financial Group, a merchant bank specialising in providing consultancy and management services to banks and financial institutions. The Group worked with experts from the New York law firm, Wachtell, Lipton, Rosen & Katz doing bank investigations.

Ludwig had since become a global fireman for banks in trouble. This was his second case where a foreign bank had suffered a catastrophic loss at a wholly-owned American subsidiary. In 2001 Ludwig had been called upon to review crippling write-offs at National Australia Bank's US mortgage subsidiary, HomeSide Lending. Because of internal mismanagement at HomeSide, Australia's largest bank had to write off $1.75 billion, largely from bungled interest rate hedging. The outcome would have provided some comfort for AIB. Three American executives had been fired but no one had to step down at head office. His report found no evidence that National Australia Group directors and executives were derelict in their duties. The bank's chief executive, who called the losses 'a disaster', did not have to resign. National Australia Bank later concluded that it was not such a good idea to have an operation in the United States. It sold the assets of its American mortgage unit for $1.9 billion in December 2001.

Ludwig had also gained a reputation as a leading advocate for improving world-wide regulatory standards. Just over a year earlier he had warned, 'Unless we make serious progress towards updating, promulgating and enforcing international standards for the global economy, I must predict another serious international financial services debacle within the next decade.'

It had come earlier than he had predicted and what Ludwig and the legal team from New York were about to investigate would turn out to be the fourth-largest fraud in banking history.

3

The Secret Love Affair

The first hint that Allied Irish Banks would one day make a major investment in the United States came in a somewhat unorthodox manner in 1975 from the then chairman, Mon O'Driscoll, at a press conference in London.

Just beforehand, AIB press officer, Bob Ryan, cautioned O'Driscoll that a Press Association reporter, Gerald Luke, was planning to ask him if AIB would follow its expansion into the United Kingdom with a similar venture in North America. 'No, we haven't decided that at all, our concentration is the UK,' O'Driscoll told Ryan. But when Luke later asked the question, the AIB chairman stunned his fellow bankers – and directors back in Ireland – by declaring boldly, 'Yes, we'll be there before the year's out.'

The story was splashed across the front pages of the Irish newspapers. At AIB's Dublin headquarters there was consternation. A senior official in the executive offices, Jeremiah Casey, anxiously asked Ryan, 'Tell me, has anyone any files on North America?' There were none, was the reply.

AIB soon afterwards sent a bank official called Wyndham W Williams to open a representative office in New York to establish the bank's presence in the United States without doing any actual banking business. He was a larger-than-life character and made such an impression that he would be remembered in New York years later. But he did not do any banking.

After two years AIB decided to go ahead and open a full branch office. Williams returned to Dublin and Jerry Casey was sent to New York. He acquired a licence to operate a bank and premises at 405 Park Avenue near the Waldorf Hotel.

AIB had at the same time begun an intensive survey to determine where it could invest most profitably abroad. The bank was doing very well and had a powerful cash flow despite the depressed economic climate in the Republic, and there were no suitable re-investment opportunities in Ireland. Paddy Dowling, deputy chief executive, did a study of the possibility of taking over a foreign bank. Morgan Guaranty Financial Services Group was asked to suggest an attractive partner in the United States where the banking system was well established and regulated. There was considerable clarity of strategic vision in the proposal to buy a bank on the other side of the Atlantic. In 1983 there was a very rigid banking system in the United States. There was little interstate banking. But Patrick O'Keefe, the new CEO of the Irish bank, an imposing banker known internally as the 'Big White Chief' and Gerald B Scanlan, soon to succeed Patrick O'Keefe as AIB chief executive, reckoned that one day the regulated American environment would change. So in 1983 they set out to acquire for AIB 'a ticket for what was going to be the biggest game in town.' The game would be acquisitions and mergers, with the prospect of an AIB-owned bank in America growing ever bigger and richer.

The bank wanted to spread its wings 'geographically as well as through a diversification in currency base,' explained Niall Crowley, who had taken over from Mon O'Driscoll as AIB chairman. He believed that with the world's strongest economy, the United States was the best place to encourage capital growth. 'We sought a partnership under the most friendly of terms,' Crowley said. 'We looked for a bank with a solid profit record, with good management, with no significant prob-lems, and with an asset and deposit size compatible with our own.'

Baltimore looked like a likely location. Lying just south of the Mason-Dixon Line at the head of Chesapeake Bay, the city's com-mercial ties were with the north though its emotional ties were with the south. It was the most northerly of southern cities and the most southerly of northern cities. It was an important port close to Washington and suited to economic development, and easily within reach of Dublin. The people spoke English, though the Irish bankers would learn that 'Murlin' meant Maryland and 'payment' meant the hard surface of a road. Most importantly there were scores of banks in Maryland and the surrounding states that would be consolidating in the years to come. Crowley also expressed the opinion that Ireland had a particular cultural and commercial affinity with the state of Maryland, whose population did not differ greatly from that of Ireland.

Baltimore was not an Irish-American metropolis like Boston, but did have strong Irish connections. The two largest ethnic groups of European origin to settle in the city were the Germans and the Irish, and the Irish had retained their identity to a greater degree. The Basilica of the Assumption of the Blessed Virgin Mary, America's first Catholic cathedral, was founded by America's first Catholic Bishop, John Carroll, who came from a prominent Irish-American family. In the 1980 census, 17.4 per cent of the population declared itself to be Irish in origin. The city held a big St Patrick's Day parade every year. (Today its 39-year-old Irish-American mayor, Martin O'Malley, is the front man for an Irish rock band, 'O'Malley's March'.)

In Baltimore, one of the most important and well-run banks was by happy coincidence at the same time looking overseas for a European bank to come and form a partnership. First National Bank of Maryland needed rescuing from a dilemma caused by the fact that while successful, it might not be able to resist a 'hostile' takeover by an American bank.

The First Maryland Chairman, J Owen Cole, a cautious banker who preferred to carry strategic planning in his head rather than on paper, had embarked on a series of takeovers of smaller banks in Maryland, convinced that First Maryland had to be present in every part of the state to become big enough to remain on its own feet. During an aggressive five-year expansion First Maryland had acquired no less than ten smaller banks, giving it total assets of $3.65 billion and 166 branches in Maryland, Washington DC, northern Virginia, Delaware and Pennsylvania. This confirmed First Maryland as the second-biggest bank in Maryland, but it was still vulnerable. It needed a new partner to reinforce its capital base with new money after a slump in South American economies where it had significant exposure. The executives fretted that if the publicly-held Baltimore company was acquired by a bigger American bank they would all be replaced by a new management team – that was the way bank takeovers usually worked in the United States – and relegated to the status of a regional outlet. The system was brutal. If an American owner came in they could all be fired.

The ideal solution was finding an owner 'thousands of miles away, not too large, with a management that spoke English, that would allow First Maryland, assuming that it performed well, to keep its

name and management,' said a former senior executive at First
Maryland. 'That was at the top of our wish list – and lo and behold,
AIB approached from New York.'

First Maryland was nearly as old as Baltimore itself. It started out as
the Mechanics Bank in 1806 with paid-in capital of $640,000 and a
constitution which stipulated that nine of its twelve directors should
be practical mechanics or manufacturers. In 1864 the Mechanics Bank
was made national under the National Bank Act, which regularised
the United States currency. It was renamed the First National Bank
of Maryland and it flourished as Baltimore boomed with an influx of
new immigrants from Germany, Ireland, Poland, Italy and Russia.

Its headquarters at the corner of South and German Streets
burned down in the Great Baltimore Fire of 7 February 1904.
However, the minutes of the directors' emergency meeting six days
later recorded that 'the vaults of this bank remained intact and that
safes containing cash and securities were found in absolutely perfect
condition; the building alone being lost, and that well-insured.'

In 1913 First National Bank of Maryland merged with the
Merchants Bank, another venerable Baltimore institution whose
leaders included Johns Hopkins, benefactor of the university and
hospital that today bear his name. It copper-fastened its reputation
as a solid business bank. Even during the Great Depression it continued paying dividends to shareholders. 'They didn't call in loans
during the Depression,' recalled Marc Blum, a Baltimore lawyer
whose family owned a famous Baltimore department store.

First National Bank of Maryland was considered a blue-blood,
Anglophile institution in Baltimore, where most of the executives
were Protestants, with the notable exception of one of the four executive vice-presidents, Joe Peters, who was a Catholic. Baltimore's
'blue-bloods' were like the New England Brahmins. The city still had
a Blue Book listing those on the social 'A-list', families that tended
to have long pedigrees, though the number of debutantes listed as
candidates for 'coming out' at Baltimore's annual Bachelors'
Cotillion, had declined in recent years.

First Maryland's rival and the state's biggest bank by far, Maryland
National (MNC), was known as the Catholic bank. Maryland has a
strong Catholic tradition which began in 1634 when about two
hundred Catholic settlers arrived from England, fleeing penal laws.

George Calvert, the first Lord Baltimore, planned Maryland as a refuge for Catholics forbidden to practice in England. In 1704 the Royal Governor, John Seymour, promulgated an 'Act to Prevent the Growth of Popery' but the Maryland Catholic tradition endured.

First National Bank of Maryland – or First Maryland as many people called it for short – moved in 1972 to a twenty-two-storey office block at 25 South Charles Street, near where the inner harbour complex of pavilions, shops and restaurants would be built in the next decade. In a city which boasted several firsts – the first manned balloon flight, the first investment bank in America, the first electric refrigerator, the first drive-in petrol station and the first strip shopping centre – the bank could boast several 'firsts' of its own. These included the first credit cards with pictures and the first ATM machines in Maryland. It managed federal funds for smaller banks like Equitable and Mercantile and several big public funds, and by 1983 had become the premier public funds bank in the state. The bank had made a serious attempt to get into the retail market, though this was proving difficult as other banks had snapped up the best street locations, leaving First Maryland with the left-overs.

AIB approached First Maryland and negotiations got under way. The bank was attractive to the Irish as it was very conservative and prudent in its approach to lending. Executives from both sides carried on what a First Maryland vice-president called a 'secret love affair' for some weeks. J Owen Cole and the president of First Maryland, Charles W Cole, Jr (no relation) and other top people were flown to Dublin and put up in the Berkeley Court Hotel for hush-hush meetings with Patrick O'Keefe and Gerry Scanlan. In the eyes of the Baltimore contingent, Scanlan was the real architect of the deal. Jerry Casey was also brought into the negotiations.

On 7 March 1983 both banks announced an agreement under which AIB would take a majority shareholding in First Maryland with the aim of buying it out within five years. The American bank staff at 25 South Charles Street were stunned when they heard the news. One executive recalled that the reaction was at first shock, then that 'it could be worse, it could be the Germans or the Japanese.' Rival banks in Maryland were caught flat-footed.

In Dublin there was joy at AIB. The acquisition of an American bank would enable it to leapfrog its main rival, Bank of Ireland, for long the dominant bank in the Republic. A former AIB regional manager remembered, 'I was elated. We all were. It was very good for morale. It put the kybosh on the Bank of Ireland.'

In time some of the First Maryland executives would speculate bitterly that it was a mistake and, after all, unnecessary. 'Mercantile down the street is doing fine,' said a former vice-president years later, referring to a rival that had avoided any takeover and had expanded steadily to become the biggest locally-owned bank in Maryland. But the Baltimore bankers were delighted at the time. Most foreign-owned banks in the United States were extensions of their parent banks overseas, and usually carried the same name. Under the AIB deal, however, First Maryland would retain its own name, management and business plan, while enjoying an influx of new capital. First Maryland would have a representative on AIB's board and four people from AIB would sit on the Maryland board.

J Owen Cole and Charlie Cole assured staff and shareholders, in a joint statement, that while Allied Irish Banks had become the major stockholder with a view to outright acquisition, First Maryland 'will retain its identity and management.' This was crucial to their understanding of the deal, that the new owner would let them continue operating as before, though the agreement noted that future appointments to chief executive 'shall require the prior written approval of AIB'. The combination of the domestic and international banking experience of this company and of Allied Irish Banks 'will result in a truly dynamic, competitive and innovative financial services entity,' the two Baltimore bankers declared. The glossy cover of the bank's annual report for 1983 showed yachts in full sail with the words: 'In the Chesapeake Bay Country, favourable Irish winds have strengthened First Maryland's position.'

Under the agreement, put into effect just before Christmas 1983, Allied Irish Banks effectively gave itself five years to decide whether to buy the bank outright. It initially bought 1.8 million shares from First Maryland's stockholders at $35 per share, and presented First Maryland with $32 million as payment for 800,000 newly-issued shares, at a total cost to AIB of $95 million. This gave it a majority but not a controlling interest. AIB undertook to buy an additional 250,000 shares each year from 1983 to 1987, keeping its stake below 50 per cent to give First Maryland flexibility regarding regional alliances and to keep its own options open. It would then decide whether to fish or cut bait and make an outright acquisition of the American bank.

The First Maryland board was expanded to include Jerry Casey, Niall Crowley, Paddy O'Keefe and AIB deputy chairman, Liam St John Devlin. AIB executives began travelling routinely to Baltimore to get detailed explanations of what First Maryland was doing and to emphasise the importance of strategic planning. Otherwise the two Coles were given a free hand to get on with running the bank. 'We didn't want to bring in a team from Ireland to run the bank,' said Casey later. 'We didn't feel banking skills were transplantable.'

Jerry Casey left New York to take up permanent residence in Baltimore as a member of First Maryland's board, and with the title of AIB group general manager in the United States. He was to be the key link between the two banks. It was a challenging assignment for the Cork man to be the representative of a large foreign shareholder in an American bank. Jerry Casey was a career banker, a term used in Ireland to describe an employee who joined the bank after secondary school and progressed through the branch network, gaining more knowledge of core business than someone imported from another company, but often having their experience limited to a narrow retail focus.

He was the second son of a family of seven boys. His father owned the Black Swan bar and an adjoining shop opposite City Hall in Cork. He died when Jerry was sixteen. Jerry's elder brother also died and he and the younger boys helped their mother in running the business. All the brothers became successful businessmen. After leaving Christian Brothers College in Patrick's Place, Cork, in 1955 Casey joined the Munster & Leinster Bank, which later amalgamated with two other banks to form AIB. The Munster & Leinster, head-quartered in Cork, was known as Ireland's Catholic nationalist bank. In those days officials were encouraged to go on Catholic retreats organised by the bank. Its reputation as a Catholic institution was underlined by the decision of the Vatican at the height of the Cold War to send some of its gold to the Munster & Leinster vaults for safekeeping, according to former M & L official, Bob Ryan.

Casey's first posting was to Killarney. He worked in the famous County Kerry tourist spot for a year before being posted back to Cork where he married Sally White, a fellow Munster & Leinster bank official. He took to rugby and captained the Old Christians team, and played centre and wing forward for Dolphin where he is remembered as a 'good sport' and a 'useful player'. In 1969 Casey was transferred to Dublin to work in the chairman's office, a sure sign that he was a rising star. When he was sent to New York to set up and manage AIB's first US branch office in Park Avenue, he was given the title of executive vice-president of AIB Group - North America. 'Coming out here was a gamble in the first place,' he told the *American Banker*, the newspaper of the American banking industry, in a 7 June 1991 interview. 'When I first came (to New York) in 1977, we had no licence, no premises and no staff.' He struck New York's Irish business community as reserved and conservative, in contrast to his colourful predecessor. 'He wouldn't be coming to work in Bermuda shorts,' said an acquaintance drily. His ambition was to expand the bank's scope in the United States beyond Irish America, looking to corporate America rather than ethnic Irish business.

He had personal misgivings about committing his wife and four children to a longer stay in the United States when transferring to Baltimore after four years in New York. 'I sometimes have to ask myself whether I was really entitled to transplant them and cut them off from their roots,' he said. The Caseys moved into a house with four acres outside Baltimore. The couple joined the Baltimore Country Club in Timonium, a fashionable northern suburb. Both were keen golfers: Sally once played a round with Greg Norman. Jerry Casey joined the board of Catholic Charities of the Archdiocese and got involved in Catholic Church activities, including the visit of Pope John Paul II to the city in 1995, and later received the papal honour of *Pro Ecclesia et Pontifice*.

At the bank Casey was assigned a window office on the executive twenty-second floor. His presence ensured that when AIB came to decide whether to purchase the bank outright, it would know everything about the institution from the inside. Casey liked to joke later that the step-by-step acquisition of First Maryland was 'one of the longest due diligences on record.'

Casey made an effort to fit in at First Maryland, doing the rounds and introducing himself to the senior officers. His manner was very formal: at a dinner to introduce himself to senior management on the executive floor he spoke from notes. On a personal level he was well received at first but his new American colleagues sensed a reserve. He tended to stay a little separate.

It was not easy for Casey. He was coming into a banking culture very different to the one in which he had been groomed. He was a representative of the bank's new owners but he had no real executive role. He had managed an AIB branch in New York but had no experience of how an independent American bank was run. Most of his new colleagues had spent their whole careers working and growing together in First Maryland.

'The executive vice-presidents were hardened professionals, cohesive and local, they knew what it was all about, they had dirt under their fingernails,' said a close observer. 'Casey essentially had no experience on the business side of running a bank. His headquarters career had been as executive assistant. He had been like a chamberlain to the throne.'

When AIB executives came in delegations from Dublin they golfed with their Baltimore counterparts. Their wives were brought to the city's new shopping malls. First Maryland officials who performed well during the year were flown first-class to Dublin for 'get-to-know-you' seminars with their counterparts. The Americans called the trips 'boondoggles', emphasising their social nature. But there were awkward differences in banking culture between Ireland and Maryland. AIB was a unionised bank, with a 'them and us' attitude which had once resulted in a spectacular nation-wide strike. In the Baltimore bank no one belonged to a union and cashiers or porters could be hired and fired at will, though there was often less of a demarcation between management and staff. The First Maryland bankers rightly or wrongly felt that one had to be a Catholic to get on in AIB and that the promotion path was very political. Irish executives were not as tuned-in to investing as the Americans. The Irish bank was also seen as a male preserve. 'Here we love women,' quipped a former First Maryland officer, who believed that political correctness was not well developed in Ireland. There was some amusement when an AIB internal video was screened for staff in Baltimore, showing mandatory new uniforms for female staff. 'I recall that it had women on a runway in these uniforms to the music of Al Green's "I'm So in Love with You",' said a staff member who saw it.

'The women executives hated it. One made the point that the men were not told to wear uniforms.'

The Irish for their part felt that the American executives were taking too much out of the bank in the form of compensation and stock options. US banking salaries were much higher than those in Dublin. Gerry Scanlan would bring the matter up at board meetings. A veteran AIB man said, 'These guys were past masters at stock options and such like. They were making huge money.' 'The pay issue was a sore spot with the Irish,' said a former American executive vice-president. 'We always got the vibes that we were over-compensated, but in Baltimore we were never the leader in compensation.'

The American bankers found the Irish system archaic. 'In Dublin they had lunch with wine, we wouldn't have anything like that, and they also closed the branches for lunch,' said the former executive vice-president. 'The Irish were very big on planning and the use of consultants but "you're not in business for the sake of the plan."' He also recalled that the Irish had a negative attitude when they came to Baltimore, then went back home and took all the credit. But on balance both sides felt it was a pretty healthy relationship.

4

Boardroom Coup

Charlie Cole became president and chief executive of First Maryland on 1 July 1984 when J Owen Cole stepped down as chief executive.

The new chief executive was highly respected in Baltimore business circles. He was a blue-blood with an old-money background. Charlie Cole was in the 'Blue Book', as were a number of First Maryland executives like Carroll Jackson, William T Murray, Tommy Swindell and Steve Sands. At one time Jackson kept a copy in the bank of the $55, members-only publication with its hard blue cover and cursive gold script which registered society marriages and deaths and the winter and summer addresses of the area's gentry. Cole was also a member and president for many years of the Elkridge Club on Charles Street, which had exacting entrance requirements and a restricted membership. 'It is the most exclusive club in the area,' said a retired banker. 'You don't have to be in the Blue Book to belong but I'd bet money that just about everybody who is in the Blue Book does belong.' Membership of the Elkridge Club was highly valued in a city where high society was said to be as 'closed' as in Charleston, South Carolina. Cole held a 'goose dinner' in the club every Christmas for his senior management.

Charlie Cole was angular and thin with a courtly manner, and a passion for tennis. He organised First Maryland sponsorship for tennis tournaments and was pictured with his arms around Baltimore's tennis star Pam Shriver and Martina Navratilova in the bank's 1986 annual report. He was good with people and at bringing in new custom. He was totally dedicated to the bank, always out looking for new business. It was said that if anything moved in Baltimore, Charlie had his finger in it.

Cole was first into the bank in the morning, sometimes as early as 6.00 am, after rising at 4.00 am to do exercises at home. He was plagued by a back injury, which got so painful he sometimes had to stand during meetings. When his colleagues arrived into work they found that Cole had read every business and financial newspaper, giving him an edge in the bank's investment operations, his great strength. He disapproved of anyone smoking in or out of the office and was appalled when AIB executives arrived for board meetings puffing cigarettes.

'Charlie Cole is a careful, thorough, sober kind of guy who touches bases, he's a disciplined and aware banker,' said lawyer Marc Blum. He liked to treat the bank staff as family. When an official was fired for making a mistake, she was accepted back to a new job in the bank and greeted with a slide from Cole saying: 'Welcome back to the family.'

Charlie's high-level connections in Maryland society proved vital for AIB's precarious toe-hold in American banking. There was no nation-wide banking in the United States at that time and Maryland Governor, Harry Hughes, set up a committee on interstate banking that in 1984 proposed a bill to enable the state's eighty-nine banks to participate in an interstate compact with fifteen other southern states. But a provision in the bill would bar foreign-owned banks from purchasing Maryland institutions. This was 'straight-out discrimination', Cole told the *American Banker*. He said it would signal to the world that Maryland was not interested in foreign investment. AIB would not have invested in First Maryland if such a law was on the books.

Cole, who had a law degree, lobbied for an amendment that any foreign bank that made Maryland its 'home state' as defined by federal law would be treated the same as other Maryland banks. This was regarded as a declaration of war by the four main rival banks, MNC, Equitable, Union, and Mercantile Bankshares. They argued for the exclusion of foreign bank acquisitions, saying that it was unfair if a Maryland bank, which was a subsidiary of a foreign parent bank, was allowed to acquire a bank in another state, if the target bank could not acquire the Maryland bank because of its foreign ownership.

It was a stressful time for Cole who made several trips to the state capital Annapolis to lobby legislators and the governor, with whom he was friendly. A blue-ribbon commission was set up in Baltimore composed of ten local corporate leaders to decide the issue. In a room packed with media and officials, the CEOs of the four rival banks made their case and Charlie Cole argued forcefully for a level playing field. He won hands down. The battle was so personal, however, that to this day, the then chairman of Mercantile, H Furlong Baldwin, does not speak to Charlie Cole.

AIB later designated Maryland as its 'home state' in the US, so that its expansion in the region would be subject to the same conditions as applied to domestic banks in the same state. The passing of reciprocal banking laws made First Maryland's charter much more valuable for AIB. It was an important victory for the Irish in a legislative fight for AIB's right to buy First Maryland outright and to be treated on equal terms with American-owned banks.

Then a disaster overcame the parent bank. On the eve of the long St Patrick's weekend in 1985, AIB announced that it had asked the government to take over its wholly-owned Insurance Corporation of Ireland (ICI) to prevent a collapse of the bank and possibly the Irish economy. It was a deeply traumatic, humiliating day, remembered by contemporary AIB employees with some degree of bitterness. AIB executives everywhere were blind-sided. The survivability of Ireland's biggest bank, which they believed to be as secure as the State itself, was suddenly in the balance.

The crisis in Ireland led to what the *Washington Post* called 'speculative frenzy' in the United States that AIB might sell its First Maryland holding. 'That is absolute rubbish,' Casey told the *Washington Post*. Allied Irish Banks was 'entirely happy with its investment in First Maryland.' He had good reason for saying so. AIB's investment of $120 million had become worth about $250 million and net income was increasing by twenty per cent a year. But Casey too had been blind-sided. After the ICI fiasco AIB staff felt let down, especially those posted far from headquarters.

In November 1985, Casey became vice-chairman of First Maryland, with the agreement of Charlie Cole and J Owen Cole. In doing so the Cork man severed his employment contract with AIB and became a lot more independent from the parent bank, a decision which was greeted with some dismay, even anger, among his AIB colleagues back home. With AIB going through uncertain times, the move provided the banker from Cork with bullet-proof employment and made him wealthy by Irish banking standards. It gave him access to the First Maryland stock programme, a salary and compensation level commensurate with American banking management, and a pension based on his years in AIB.

First Maryland had a restricted stock programme under which top executives got shares that they could cash a number of years in the future, as an incentive for them to stay with the bank. It was a system of 'golden handcuffs'. Restrictions on receiving and selling the stock lapsed in equal amounts on the third, fourth and fifth anniversaries of each respective grant. (In 1993, for example, Casey would get $525,000 in restricted stock awards.) These were different from stock options which depended on the stock price rising. They were guaranteed payments. This type of compensation was then unknown in Ireland; modest awards of restricted stock made their first appearance at AIB in 2001.

The new management arrangement appeared to suit everyone. Charlie Cole still had the bank to run, and Casey was a minister without portfolio, having influence without interference.

Three years later, in June 1987, J Owen Cole gave up his remaining role as chairman and left the bank. Charlie Cole gathered his four executive vice-presidents, Joseph E Peters, Frederick W Meier Jr, William T Murray III, and Robert W Schaefer in Peters' office to tell them that AIB had decided that Jerry Casey should be the next chairman. This was a break with long-standing First Maryland tradition where promotion to the top came from within and the chief executive eventually became chairman, allowing one of the four executive vice-presidents a shot at the CEO job. Joe Peters, the favourite to succeed Cole, felt it was a horrible decision for the Irish to make as it blocked the natural progression to the top.

There was now an Irishman and an American in each of the two top positions in the Baltimore bank, with Casey representing the majority shareholder as chairman and Charlie Cole running the bank as president and chief executive, along with his elite group of four American executive vice-presidents. 'The appointment of Casey suggests that Allied Irish is preparing to assume a more active role in directing the fortunes of Maryland's second-largest bank company,' said the *Washington Post*. 'Casey's election as chairman certainly appears to herald a new era.'

Despite the bank's steady earning performance, relations between Charlie Cole and Jerry Casey cooled considerably as time went by. People around Cole felt that the AIB man was trying to take over the running of the bank and propel it in directions which they disapproved of. Casey became quite isolated in his corner office on the executive twenty-second floor. He was up against what a former First Maryland executive frankly described as 'our little in-bred group which had been working together in the bank for a long time.'

Only one American bank executive got close to the Cork man. This was Brian L King, the senior vice-president in charge of personnel and a former helicopter pilot in the US Army. He had a reputation as a meticulous note-keeper, like J Edgar Hoover, with files on everything. The two had long conversations in Casey's office. Colleagues resented King's closeness to the new chairman, seeing it as a political career decision. An atmosphere of suspicion and intrigue developed on the twenty-second floor.

Five years after taking a stake in First Maryland, AIB had to make up its mind whether to acquire First Maryland outright. It had to decide whether to bid for the balance or sell, to move from passive investor or to get out. There was a lot of soul-searching in Dublin. Both Charlie Cole and Jerry Casey had been elected members of the AIB board in Dublin. When it came time for the AIB board to deliberate its decision, both stepped down as directors because of their direct interest.

It was touch and go. The arguments went back and forth in the AIB boardroom. Some had the view that First Maryland had not really done an awful lot, despite the solid earnings performance, and that it was too remote. It had not made any significant acquisitions. The more popular view was that they could make it work. The AIB board decided to buy First Maryland outright but it was a split view and the indecision meant that the deal wasn't completed until 1989, a year behind schedule.

To the surprise of many, Cole and Casey were not invited back onto the AIB board after the decision was taken. Casey was, however, appointed chief executive in the USA, making the Cork man part of the AIB family once more. Cole was not unhappy about leaving the AIB board. He had been complaining to friends that the monthly trips to Dublin via London were taking him away from running the bank and watching his beloved bond markets.

The takeover was completed in March 1989 when AIB raised its stake to 100 per cent of the stock, making First Maryland a component but autonomous part of Ireland's biggest bank. The total AIB investment was approximately $150 million, of which more than $80 million went to First Maryland as new capital and the rest to First Maryland stockholders, most of them residents of Maryland.

The antipathy between the chairman and chief executive was by now seen as deeply personal. But strategic planning was a real issue of contention between them. Maryland executives recall that Casey wanted to transform the institution into more of a retail than a business-oriented bank. He wanted to expand by acquiring retail banks like Dauphin Deposit in Pennsylvania. Cole also wanted to expand but had in mind buying a business operation like an asset management company rather than a retail bank, but Casey and Dublin would have none of that.

Charlie Cole had kept strategic and tactical planning but after the buy-out in 1989 Casey succeeded in getting strategic planning to himself.

Jerry Casey's first serious attempt to buy another financial institution earned him a footnote in US banking history as the first foreign banker to make a hostile takeover bid for an American bank. His target was Baltimore Bancorp, with $3.4 billion in assets and 51 branches. A merger would give First Maryland a total of $10.6 billion in assets and about two hundred branches, fortifying its position as the second-largest Maryland bank company. On Friday 27 April 1990, Casey had a letter delivered without prior warning to Harry W Robinson, Baltimore Bancorp's chairman and chief executive, and to the firm's directors, offering 'in a spirit of cordiality and goodwill' to buy Baltimore Bancorp at $17 a share, well above the market price. He said he wanted an answer by the following Wednesday, 2 May. The offer was simultaneously announced to the media.

Robinson was furious. On Monday the Baltimore Bancorp boss released his reply. He took issue with the notion that the offer was delivered in a 'spirit of cordiality and goodwill', he said. 'The approach of delivering an offer to me and my directors on a Friday afternoon, before even having the courtesy to telephone me; the suggestion of a May 2nd deadline for a response; and your immediate distribution of a press release could only have been designed to create a hostile atmosphere and to place pressure on us. Please rest assured we will not be cowed by these tactics.' Noting that there was no commitment by AIB to retain staff at Baltimore Bancorp he said, 'This suggests the slash and burn technique of the hostile raider.'

Cole was against the bid for Baltimore Bancorp, as were the majority of the executive vice-presidents. The chief executive said he preferred quality over quantity and if they landed themselves with a bunch of bad assets it would ruin everything. Casey was adamant he wanted the acquisition. Four weeks later, in a new approach to Robinson, Casey said an increased bid would be considered if due diligence – an inspection of Baltimore Bancorp's books – confirmed a higher valuation. He said it would be conducted with any safe-guards Baltimore Bancorp required to preserve confidentiality, and he repeated that his rejected offer was of 'fair and full value.'

Robinson ignored Casey and wrote directly to AIB in Dublin. The proposed higher offer following due diligence was 'of no interest' to him, he said. Moreover there were concerns over secrecy. No confidentiality agreement could completely allay anxieties about rival First Maryland inspecting its books. 'We see no reason to revisit our original decision.' First Maryland did, however, get to do due diligence on Baltimore Bancorp and Casey quickly dropped his takeover bid when it was found to be in a mess, with real estate loan problems.

Casey still believed, however, that it was a good time to buy solid US banks. 'He was hell bent on acquisition,' recalled a First Maryland veteran who had supported Casey on the Baltimore Bancorp bid. 'Expanding our territory made some sense at the right price, though I was in the minority.'

Casey was more successful with two other attempted acquisitions. First Maryland bought the tiny Columbia National Bank in Washington with $22 million in assets and in May 1991 he made a successful bid for York Bank, a 180-year-old commercial and com-munity bank based in York, Pennsylvania with $1.4 billion in assets. Casey said at the time that it was part of the company's strategy to expand into states around Maryland and that more acquisitions were being studied. The annual report that year described the acquisition of York Bank as a 'natural, contiguous expansion within our targeted market and in keeping with our strategic objectives.' Casey also pointed out that because of its image as a strongly capitalised bank,

First Maryland had gained over $1 billion in deposits in 1990.

Charlie Cole was unhappy with the decision to acquire York. He argued that it was too costly an acquisition. Cole's allies felt that Jerry Casey was anxious to show expansion in addition to organic growth to improve his prospect of eventual promotion to the top job in Dublin, which was soon to become vacant. As the rift between Cole and Casey widened, small things began to take on great significance. One of these was the gold quality lapel pin.

Charlie Cole had a team approach to management. People from different departments were required to meet regularly to discuss policy issues like margin analysis, retail and corporate marketing, and information technology. One group was called the Total Quality Committee, which was charged with improving service standards. It came up with the idea that all 1,000 First Maryland employees, even the executives, should wear a gold lapel pin bearing the word 'Quality', to emphasise that the culture of the bank was to provide a quality service and a good product. Cole embraced this scheme enthusiastically. He preferred quality over quantity. Staffers noted, however, that Jerry Casey didn't wear the pin.

The situation on the twenty-second floor deteriorated to the point where 'Casey would bring back orders from Ireland and Charlie would just ignore them,' said a senior staff member. Things became so strained that 'you never got Jerry and Charlie in the same room unless they had to.'

When Cole had the lobby of the executive twenty-second floor redesigned to his taste, and Casey had the boardroom – his preserve as chairman – done over, staff interpreted this as an exercise in status management. Several times over the years the walls of the top floor executive offices would be knocked down and repositioned to reflect changes in the standing of personnel, a process that seemed never-ending. 'I can't tell you how many times we redid it,' said a former executive, 'and these were expensive walls; we're not talking plywood.'

As relations worsened, Cole took comfort from the balance sheet and from what he saw as continuing support for his management from Dublin. AIB chairman, Jim Culliton, sent him a handwritten note dated 9 July 1993, saying that 'we are all very proud of what you and your colleagues have achieved at First Maryland and I can assure you of continuing support from the chair.' A First Maryland execu-tive visiting Dublin in October 1993 had a brief exchange with Tom Mulcahy, head of AIB Capital Markets Division, that was duly reported back to Cole. 'You work with Charlie?' Mulcahy had said. 'Charlie's doing a good job. We want to keep Charlie happy.' But it was noted that Cole had been invited on the same trip and had not made it. The support from Dublin was, in fact, pretty shaky. The blunt-talking Mulcahy reportedly did not relate well with the courtly American banker who resisted Dublin's interference, nor with his four American executive vice-presidents.

Casey was by now attracting the attention of the banking world in the United States. In June 1991 the *American Banker* gave him a glowing write-up. During the 'success story' of his fourteen years in the US, 'Casey has masterfully straddled the cultural divide, adjust-ing successfully to the changing American focus on business,' wrote reporter James Kraus. 'Along the way he has accumulated a fair amount of wealth for Allied Irish Banks.' Casey told Kraus, 'One of the first things you learn when you come here is that there is no such thing as a free lunch. People in the United States are obsessed with the creation and management of wealth.'

Under Charlie Cole as CEO the bank improved its earnings performance every year from 1984 to 1993, despite a recession at the beginning of the 1990s when many banks foundered. It was a star performer among the top 100 American banks. 'We could have shown 30 per cent earnings instead of 20 per cent in 1993,' said a former top executive many years later.

American colleagues felt there was a lot of depth in management under Cole. People understood what they were doing, they said, they weren't making decisions from a textbook or from trans-Atlantic flights at 35,000 feet. While the bank maintained a focus on retail, commercial lending, international, treasury, real estate and asset management, Cole's philosophy was that 'we can't be the biggest in the world so we will go for quality.' When the real estate crash came in 1990, First Maryland was one of the few American banks to remain solid, while its main rival in Baltimore, MNC, struggled to avoid collapse.

His record impressed some AIB figures who noted that he kept First Maryland profitable when three hundred banks a year were going out of business in the United States. Charlie Cole was no great enthusiast for lending and made sure the lending policies were very tight. His great skill was as a player in the bond market. He actively traded bonds all day long, which was very important for the bank's business, and he was regarded as very skilful in calling long-term interest rates.

In Dublin, however, Casey was given the credit for the profit record. A profile in the *Irish Times* in January 1993 said Casey was credited with avoiding the heavy losses suffered by many US banks, through cutting back on property lending before real estate values fell sharply and with engineering a switch towards non-interest income as interest income came under pressure because of falling interest rates and loan demand. Casey did not in fact make loan decisions, former executives recalled, nor was he significantly involved in the performance of First Maryland, though he was regarded as an extremely presentable spokesman for the bank. But First Maryland executives were not unhappy about Casey getting the credit in Ireland. They hoped it would help him get the big job and he would be able to return to Dublin.

Everyone at the Baltimore bank knew that Casey had his heart set on the job of AIB chief executive. 'We all talked about it. We knew his heart was there. He had property in Dublin. He was looking forward to it. We wanted to know what are our guy's chances? If he gets the credit for First Maryland's performance, good for him if he gets the top job. He would have felt good about it and we would have someone in Dublin who knew us,' said a former executive vice-president.

Friends of Casey thought that the acquisition of York Bank made him favourite. One of the credentials of a CEO candidate was to pull off a few big deals. The consolidation game had started in the region with other banks getting bigger through acquisitions, and York Bank was the answer to critics who asked what First Maryland was doing about it.

In October 1993 Gerry Scanlan, who had been chief executive of AIB in Dublin since 1985, announced that he was retiring in March 1994. That same month Casey was re-appointed to the AIB group board. The *Irish Times* reported that 'his successful management of the US operation in difficult markets has made Mr Casey one of the prime candidates to succeed Mr Scanlan.'

Jerry Casey took a plane to Dublin to present himself as the clear favourite for the top job over Tom Mulcahy, who had come up through AIB's ranks before assuming responsibility for its highly successful foreign exchange dealing and stockbroking activities. The interview board, chaired by former AIB chairman, Peter Sutherland, was reported to be overwhelmed by Mulcahy's in-depth knowledge of every aspect of the bank and his plan to prune branches.

Mulcahy got the job.

'Jerry Casey was bitterly disappointed,' recalled a friend from his earlier AIB days. Another AIB veteran recalled that Sutherland was well-informed on the US and was 'unimpressed' by what he had seen in Baltimore.

But Mulcahy did not have a free hand as the new AIB chief executive. Almost half the board had favoured Casey. Mulcahy had campaigned on the platform of sorting out First Maryland, saying that by then it was obvious that it was not one of the participants in the consolidation game. For the first time its performance showed signs of being a bit pedestrian. There was a feeling gathering momentum in Dublin that the bank was not being run by Charlie Cole for the benefit of AIB. Mulcahy did a deal with Casey, an insider said. If Casey decided to put in a new team and revitalise First Maryland through acquisitions, then he would support him.

Jerry Casey talked by telephone with the First Maryland chief executive before returning to Baltimore. Cole was astonished by his tone and what he said. He was left with the distinct impression that Casey was angry and that his job and those of the senior managers were no longer secure, and that Casey blamed Cole for not getting the job.

When he returned from Dublin to 25 South Charles Street, Casey retreated to his office and for weeks rarely emerged, often eating alone. His attitude was very different. He was more aloof than before. The antipathy between the two top men became a test of loyalties. There was near panic among assistant staff when the brochure for the 1993 annual report was being compiled. Year after year the photographs of Cole and Casey had appeared opposite each other in the glossy annual report, each picture always exactly the same size and shape as the other, with Cole on the left side of the page and Casey on the right. The calibration was as precise and as

informative about the leaders' claim to equal status as was the
arrangement of photographs of the Communist Party politburo in
Pravda. But for some reason in the previous year's report the positions
had been reversed. What now if both men demanded the same side
of the page? A secretary acted as go-between. There was huge relief
when Cole opted for the left-hand page again and, separately, Casey
opted for the right-hand page. An awkward crisis had been averted.

While he might have spent a lot of time alone in his office, Casey
was not idle. He was laying the groundwork for the coup he and
Mulcahy had planned.

The moment for action came on the morning of 28 January 1994.
The bank's eighteen directors gathered in the boardroom on the
twenty-second floor that Thursday morning for the presentation of
the annual accounts. Tom Mulcahy was there as one of four AIB
directors. Charlie Cole gave the directors a glowing report on the
bank's progress: First Maryland had posted net income of $114
million, representing a 23 per cent increase over the previous year,
and rounding out a ten-year period during which First Maryland had
compiled a compound annual earnings growth rate in excess of
20 per cent. It had been one of the most profitable companies of any
kind in the state of Maryland. It had the best earnings record for the
previous ten years of any of the top one hundred banks in the United
States, despite a recession which had left scores of banks across the
nation bankrupt.

Just before the board meeting broke up for lunch, Cole left the
boardroom. Chief executives routinely leave board meetings when
such things as their performance or compensation is being discussed.
Shortly afterwards, according to a close friend of Cole, Casey emerged
and asked the chief executive to meet him alone in a little sitting
room, situated between the boardroom and the room where lunch
had been set out for the directors. There he told the chief executive
that he was out of a job. 'You are retiring,' he said. AIB wanted him
out. An announcement would be made that he was taking early
retirement. He had no choice in the matter. The board had decided.

Cole, a dignified man whose whole banking life had been wrapped
up in First Maryland, and who was still only 58, was shattered. The
old-money banker, a leading light in Baltimore's Blue Book and the
exclusive Elkridge Club, had been fired by an Irishman who had

started his career as a bank clerk in Killarney. He felt 'decapitated' said a friend; he was being cast out after thirty-two years at the bank, including seventeen as president and ten as chief executive.

Cole came to the lunch badly shaken but holding on to his dignity. There was, recalled one director, a 'bizarre' atmosphere. The party line was that Cole was retiring at his own suggestion.

In common with other corporate boards, the First Maryland board had several independent directors, local members of the community in good standing who brought respectability to the institution. They would be inclined to support the chief executive. But a key member, Mathias J DeVito, chairman of Rouse, a huge Maryland real estate development company, had become close to Casey. DeVito had made Casey a director of Rouse and Casey was on his compensation committee. DeVito gave crucial support to Casey in the move to oust Cole, a director said. In any event one hundred per cent control rested in the hands of the four AIB board members.

Charlie Cole left the bank that afternoon without telling his senior colleagues what had happened. Next day he came in as usual and shortly after 8.00 am he sent an official to summon staff members on the twenty-second floor to come to the boardroom. Cole walked in when everyone from catering staff (known as 'kitchen ladies') to executive vice-presidents had gathered. He told them that he was going to retire but declined to say why. There was a shocked silence. Fred Meier, one of Cole's four top men, looked sharply at all the faces around the room as if to find out who knew in advance, which might have betrayed them as disloyal to Charlie. It seemed no one knew. His closest colleagues were upset with Cole, not knowing that he had been forced out. They had all worked well together for many years. A lot of people left the meeting wondering what the rest of the story was.

On the last day of January a press release was issued by the bank announcing Cole's retirement. In it the chief executive said he was gratified to have helped position the company to take on the next wave, adding, 'Our continuing hallmark of success has been quality people producing quality assets through quality service.' Casey said that Cole could be justifiably proud of his performance in leading First Maryland to a compound annual earnings growth rate greater than 20 per cent over ten years, when assets had more than doubled from $4 billion to $9.5 billion.

Cole returned to 25 South Charles Street after a couple of weeks. He was technically not retiring until June. For a time he used the conference room as an office. There was no retirement party. He did not want one. But he made a farewell address to hundreds of staff members at the 'Sellabration', an annual pep-rally organised by Joe Peters, and held in 1994 in a large function room of the Sheraton Hotel.

'This is not going to be easy because of the high degree of emotion up here,' Cole said from the podium, before praising dozens of executives and staff by name for their work in bringing about the best results for any bank in the United States in the previous ten years. He did not mention Casey. 'At the core of First Maryland is quality, at the core of that is integrity,' he said. 'We're at half-time. The best way to lose a game is to start celebrating at half-time.'

A video of the event showed the outgoing chief executive keeping a tight control of his feelings before choking up at the end. The hundreds of bank staff gave him a prolonged standing ovation. Jerry Casey entered from stage left to honour the man he had just ousted and to convey the bank's very best wishes 'on your recent announcement.' He praised Cole fulsomely, noting that in Cole's time at the bank, the number of branches had increased from 21 to 168, assets had risen from $338 million to $9.5 billion and the loan book had gone up from $136 million to $5 billion.

'Quite frankly we all take pride in the 20 per cent compound growth rate and we all enjoy basking in that sunshine of your achievement,' he said, turning to Charlie Cole. 'We thank you for bringing us to this splendid state.' Then they shook hands. But no one mentioned publicly at the event why Charlie Cole was leaving.

Around Baltimore, people who did not know Cole assumed he was leaving while he was ahead. A local business news-sheet, *Warfield's Business Record*, compared his retirement to that of basketball star, Michael Jordan. 'The truly great leave at their peak,' it said. Cole's 'retirement' was officially recorded in a postscript by Casey inserted into the First Maryland annual report for 1993, after a joint letter in the report signed by himself and Cole. It said: 'Subsequent to the drafting of this letter, Charlie Cole announced his intention to retire from First Maryland Bancorp, effective June 30th, 1994.' A filing with the Securities & Exchange Commission (SEC) showed that Cole left with $2.1 million compensation.

Prominent citizens of Baltimore began to repeat rumours to top executives who thought Cole's departure would mean promotion for one of them. 'Have you heard your new boss is to be Frank Bramble?' Executive vice-president, Joe Peters, who headed retail banking also heard the reports. He was always the favourite to succeed Cole. His apprehension was confirmed when Casey called him in to say that AIB had decided that the position of president and chief executive officer was going to Frank Bramble, an outsider who had until recently worked in MNC. Though disappointed, Peters promised he would make every effort to ensure a smooth transition.

The rest of the story was now becoming clear.

5

The MNC Mafia

One of the first things that 45-year-old Frank Bramble did after he took over First Maryland as president and chief executive officer was to abolish the gold 'Quality' lapel pins that had been associated with Charlie Cole. It was an ominous sign for the old guard, many of whom to this day treasure their pins as a symbol of the good days at the bank.

Bramble was Casey's personal choice. They knew each other. Both were on the board of Catholic Charities of the Archdiocese of Baltimore. He came strongly recommended by Mathias DeVito, the Rouse chairman and director of First Maryland. A native of Baltimore, he was not from one of the old monied families that identified with First Maryland nor was he an A-list member of Baltimore's Blue Book.

'Bramble would have a real problem with old-money people,' said a local banker. 'Casey did, too, to a certain extent. They knew they would never be fully accepted by the people who really ran the show in Baltimore. Money will not buy you into the old-line Baltimore society. It was the Elkridge Club group that really irritated Bramble and Casey. Members of the Blue Book are not really 'visible' as opposed to members of the Elkridge Club which is very visible, especially when it comes to entertaining.' There would be no more 'goose dinners' in the Elkridge Club. Bramble was not a member. For his first Christmas party, the new chief executive would take the management team for a 'President's Dinner' to a downtown hotel; thereafter he had parties on the twenty-second floor, with a beef carving station in one room, a bar in another and lights on the fica trees. Nor would there be any more sponsorship of tennis, the sport of choice of the upper crust set. Former executives recall that that was Jerry Casey's decision.

Bramble had taken an unconventional route into banking. He did not finish college and his first job in 1966 was emptying coins from pay telephones for C&P telephone company. The next year he got a position in First National Bank of Maryland as an audit clerk but soon moved to Maryland National Bank, the main holding of MNC Financial. There he worked his way up through the ranks, from assistant and then deputy controller to vice-president of strategic planning. He left the bank in 1978 to join Danielson Associates, a new banking consultancy created by Arnold Danielson, who became a close friend. Then he ran his own bank-consulting firm for a while, before returning to MNC as vice-president of the international division.

At MNC, Bramble co-ordinated the bank's merger with American Security Corporation and Baltimore's Equitable Bancorp, making MNC a super-regional bank company. However, MNC was heading for the kind of big trouble that Charlie Cole in First Maryland had managed to avoid. MNC lent over $4 billion for commercial real estate development in the Baltimore-Washington corridor. In 1990 the commercial real estate market collapsed because of massive over-building. Bramble's bank recorded losses of $440 million in 1990 and $70 million in 1991 and came under the close supervision of the Federal Reserve and the office of the Comptroller of the Currency in Washington. 'MNC had a good façade, the guys running it were pillars of Baltimore society, but it had a rotten interior,' said a prominent Baltimore businessman.

With $4.8 billion in outstanding debt, the bank came within an ace of crashing. It was rescued by Alfred Lerner, a slight, balding former furniture salesman from Detroit with a taste for Cuban cigars, who by 1990 had become the bank's biggest shareholder and chief executive. Lerner decided that survival depended on selling the bank's assets to raise cash. 'In some cases it was literally hours before the loan payment was due that we sold the assets and got the money, it was that wild,' Bramble was to recall later.

The regulators demurred when Lerner tried to sell off one of the bank's biggest assets, its $7 billion credit card subsidiary known as MBNA. They wanted claims on it if the bank failed. Lerner forced them to back off by scribbling out a press statement declaring MNC bankrupt, something the regulators did not want. The press statement did not have to be released and now hangs framed in Lerner's office. However, no one seemed interested in buying the credit card operation and Lerner decided to sell MBNA to the public instead. The public offering was a huge success and made the Detroit business-man a billionaire. Today MBNA is the world's largest independent credit-card issuer.

Though reeling on the verge of bankruptcy, in December 1990 MNC awarded a total of $1.5 million in bonuses to senior executives (including Frank Bramble, who was then chief operating officer for the bank's two subsidiaries) while at the same time directors were cancelling fourth-quarter dividend payments to shareholders. The regulators were furious and forced the executives to give the money back. 'It was completely unacceptable and imprudent given the financial condition of the bank,' said an official of the Office of the Comptroller of the Currency.

In July 1991 Lerner gave the chief executive job to Bramble, who had reportedly encouraged him to take the credit card division public. The cost-cutting and sale of assets continued under Bramble and vice-president Peter Gartman, a *tae kwon do* expert and special-ist in corporate turnarounds. Branches were closed, more than 3,000 jobs cut and the bank virtually stopped making new loans.

MNC was still saddled with more than $1.2 billion in non-performing loans and under regulatory supervision when a year later, in July 1992, it was bought out by NationsBank of Charlotte, North Carolina. The deal 'ensures our survival,' said a relieved Lerner. Bramble called it a 'vote of confidence.' Bramble was made chairman of NationsBank's Maryland division after the merger, which went ahead in February the following year. In October 1993, after the acquisition was completed, NationsBank announced it was laying off 1,200 people in the Baltimore-Washington region. In the brutal way of bank mergers, Bramble's 'resignation' was announced two months later, in December. He said he was leaving 'to take a little time off'.

Four weeks after Bramble left MNC, Jerry Casey asked Charlie Cole to retire as president and chief executive of First Maryland and just over a month after that, on 8 March 1994, he brought Bramble in to succeed Cole and take over the bank. Bramble had become the youngest CEO in America of a bank the size of First Maryland. For Charlie Cole the fact that someone like Bramble from MNC, a banker with no university degree and very little commercial bank experience, had taken over the bank he had served and built up all his life was particularly hard to swallow.

The city's media applauded the choice, however. A *Baltimore Sun* report on 9 March noted that Mr Bramble had helped to 'rescue' Maryland's largest bank, MNC, and said the fact that he was remaining in the city was 'welcome news to some in Baltimore's business community who feared the region would lose one of its most active civic leaders.' Jerry Casey told the newspaper that First Maryland had a well established team and that there was no reason to expect a stampede of former MNC executives to First Maryland. It was clear that Casey expected Bramble to be more responsive to his leadership and that he would be able to take a more assertive role in the bank's strategy. The Irish chairman became much more 'visible' in the bank. He made it clear that First Maryland would start looking around for likely banks to buy. 'We intend to supplement our organic growth by acquisition.'

It was evident that the AIB man with roots in Cork was much more comfortable with the man from the MNC bank. It showed in little ways. Casey and Cole had never been pictured together in any First Maryland annual report during the ten years that they had held the top two positions. The photographs were always carried separately. In First Maryland's first annual report after the coup, Casey and Bramble were pictured smiling happily together in one single snapshot, like best buddies.

The stampede that Casey had said would not take place soon began, as Bramble started bringing in his own people from MNC Financial. They came in calling themselves the MNC mafia. Some staff at First Maryland referred to the newcomers as the 'Big Yahoos from MNC' who 'wanted to show us what banking was all about.' First Maryland staff saw MNC as the 'Barbarians at the Gate'. To them, MNC culture was aggressive and ruthless compared to a First Maryland culture which emphasised 'politeness, promotion from within, familiar atmosphere, respect for executive management, mutual respect, camaraderie, a co-operative rather than competitive environment and lack of ostentation.' The difference between the two banks was summed up by a former vice-president who said, 'MNC drank liquor, we had sherry.'

One of the first to go was executive vice-president, Joe Peters. Bramble told him on their first meeting that he would not be bringing in his own people to run the bank. But shortly afterwards Casey and Bramble confronted the 56-year-old Peters with the news that they were re-organising management and in spite of his record and his knowledge of the bank, there was no room for him on the new team. Though well compensated, he found the manner of his firing personally hurtful. He was going to leave anyway, but he wanted to be the one to pull the trigger.

Bill Murray, 63, another of Cole's executive vice-presidents who ran the trust department and all of the bank's operational areas was retired in similar fashion. Murray had spent his whole career at the bank and had been executive vice-president since the 1970s. A small retirement party was organised for him by senior vice-president, Charlie Siegmann. Colleagues wanted to present the retiring banker with a picture of ships from his office that he liked. It had been a tradition at First Maryland that a retiring top official could be given something to remind him of the bank. But these were different days. The bank had the picture valued and they had to chip in to buy it, said one of the organisers. It was meant to be a small affair in a restaurant outside town with none of the old or new bank leaders present. Charlie Cole heard about it and said he would like to come. 'Then a telephone call came from Jerry Casey's secretary, to say that Mr Casey assumed his invitation was in the mail,' said a former executive. 'Suddenly it had got very political.' At the party Cole and Casey barely spoke.

(Cole wanted to take three Trillingham pictures from his office that he had purchased for the bank in Bermuda and that he particularly liked, but the bank refused to sell them. Cole distributed the pictures to other executives to hang in their offices before leaving. When he had gone, workers arrived to take them back.)

In the early days Bramble held 'town hall' meetings in hotel function rooms to introduce himself to the staff at First Maryland. At these meetings he made much of his beginnings as a collector of coins from telephone boxes. He went through everything that was wrong with the bank. Expenses were too high for a bank of its size, and the company must embark on an expansion drive. His 'corporate vision' was to 'realize our potential to become the best banking company in the marketplace'. Cost-income ratio was, in fact, high at First Maryland, leaving room for some trimming.

Bramble produced a written mantra of 'corporate attitudes' for the First Maryland staff. They would 'RELENTLESSLEY ANTICIPATE and satisfy customer needs, DEMAND the best of ourselves, INSIST on teamwork and mutual respect, MAINTAIN a disciplined approach to risk-taking and investment (and) TRY lots of new things.'

On 2 August Bramble announced a sweeping overhaul of the executive ranks. He said his new management team would include a far greater number of executives reporting directly to him; thirteen compared to five in Cole's day. There would also be a number of new positions created, including a senior vice-president for 'continuous improvement'. (Over the next three years the number of executive vice-presidents rose from five to nine, and senior vice-presidents from forty-five to around ninety.)

The overhaul of management meant the arrival of several more of Bramble's colleagues at MNC to take up top positions at First Maryland. Bramble was dismantling the old team. 'There was a logic to that,' said a colleague. 'He didn't want anyone who was talking to Charlie Cole regularly. That's why a lot of people had to leave.'

Thomas D Fitzsimmons, Bramble's brother-in-law, took up the post of senior vice-president for long-range planning. Walter R Fatzinger Jr, who worked at MNC's subsidiary, American Security Bank in Washington, came in as new executive vice-president for Washington-area banking and the trust department. Jeffrey D Maddox was appointed executive vice-president for Maryland banking. Jerome W Evans was made executive vice-president and chief administrative officer. Michael Riley, who helped co-ordinate top management's community and non-profit activities at MNC, arrived to do the same work for Bramble and Casey.

Some of the bank's clients were unsettled at the removal of the top level of management. They felt that when a bank cut out a layer of management or froze them out of the chain of command, it was exposing itself to risk.

Bramble soon outlined a new corporate structure for First Maryland. He cited a recommendation by the consultancy firm of Deloitte & Touche which had just finished a seven-month study of the bank's operations, for the need to 'fine tune' practically all operations. Profits had been stagnant since the beginning of the year. For the first time in a decade, first and second quarter earnings at the company failed to match the prior year's numbers, which the company blamed on a one-time $5 million increase in employee retirement pensions. The priorities would be cutting operating costs, expanding retail lending and enhancing the bank's presence in Washington DC.

'We are a company that performs well, but I think we can perform better,' he said. The retail business was 'not as strong' as the corporate side and would be expanded – something Casey had urged for some time.

Some of the Deloitte & Touche recommendations were apparently ignored. If they had been acted upon the bank would have got out of lending to large corporations because there were no margins there any more, said a former executive.

Bramble and his team sold off the credit card division for $61 million as well as the mortgage company, a move that was criticised by the bank's former leaders as a way to improve the year-end numbers. They also drew down the loan-loss reserve, that is, they used cash set aside to offset bad loans, which critics likened to living off the earnings.

Under Bramble's new structure, the system of committees was abandoned, including the Total Quality Committee, which had been instituted to enhance customer service. The new chief executive discouraged staff from wearing the gold 'Quality' pins. In a memo written in October, Bramble stated: 'Clearly where quality was once an aspiration, it is now the standard.' David Conn, a staff writer for the *Baltimore Sun*, reported on 31 December 1994 that at a goodbye party for a senior vice-president, a brass clock was presented as a gift, prompting one person to shout, 'We made it out of melted-down quality pins.'

Not all of Bramble's critics disagreed with his move away from the quality campaign at a time when the most powerful institutions were taking over banks everywhere. 'It's no use being a quality bank if surrounded by sharks,' said one. 'The only way one could adapt was to expand. This is what drove AIB and Casey. Numbers meant everything, not symbols. You either grew it or got the hell out of it.'

Bramble promised in an internal memorandum to employees that his new 14-member management team would meet him at least once a week to 'plan, organize and control all the significant activities in our company.' He said that the large number of departments reporting to him made more sense than the previous hierarchy, which required more levels of communication. 'I think you need all the major disciplines of a company at hand so you can deal with all the issues.'

But morale at the bank had been shattered by the ruthless expulsions of the old successful team and the new style of management. Andrew Hiduke, human resources director and a senior vice-president for the previous five years, became the conduit for the anger and frustration in the First Maryland ranks at the changes. Hiduke submitted a memorandum to Bramble on 21 October 1994 that revealed the extent of the take-over by MNC people and described in detail the effects of what one vice-president called 'a climate of extraordinary fear, with management by threat'. 'Employees feel they are going through a revolution rather than an evolution,' he wrote in the memo. 'A significant number of MNC/NationsBank people have entered the organisation during the last sixty days. This is causing significant morale problems.' Formal procedures should be instituted to mitigate the costs associated with the rapid hiring and restructuring in progress. 'Based upon current data, a total of fifty-one net new positions were added, with pending proposals for an additional eighty-one positions in 1994 and sixty positions in 1995. At this time no formal plan exists for employee displacement to offset this staff build-up.'

Hiduke pointed out that people at a variety of levels in the organisation felt they no longer had the ability to share experience, knowledge and ideas. 'The feeling that we have been acquired by the MNC management team has been heard in several areas', the memo continued. 'The influx of MNC people at senior level has limited career potential for experienced FMB people; support of internal and external training appears to have diminished; some good people are looking for opportunities outside the bank. Failure to acknowledge the past contributions of FMB people, those still on board and those no longer here, makes it more difficult to accept the changes and move on.'

The 'high degree of uncertainty' in the bank had also affected many people's ability to focus and get enthusiastic about changes already announced, and was also impacting upon productivity and morale, Hiduke wrote. The lack of clear direction 'has left some employees feeling that there were 150 priorities which were all number 1'.

The phrase 'That's the way Maryland National did it' was getting old, he went on. There was also a perception that 'we will be moving away from our commitment to quality customer service' because of the disbanding of the Total Quality Programme. Hiduke pointed out that human resources representatives 'are hearing these concerns from people in many areas of the company and at all levels within the organisation.'

The morale problem was not confined to 25 South Charles Street headquarters. The axe was also wielded in the branches, where managers were taken out to save money, leaving the running of the branches on the cheap to their subordinates, a programme enforced by former MNC executive, Jeff Maddox.

In September 1994, four more senior vice-presidents left: Donald E Sheerer, president of First Maryland Brokerage, Richard F Barnard, head of the branch network, William P Young, in charge of commercial banking in the Washington DC area and John E Shultz who ran branch administration. In December 1994 several more senior vice-presidents left, including Gary Sutton, general counsel and corporate secretary, Alan N Siegfried, in charge of corporate auditing and William A Quade, head of commercial lending in the York Bank subsidiary. They were routinely replaced with MNC bankers. In that month five MNC bankers were hired.

Many former executives expressed particular anger about the way a well-loved and long-serving vice-president, Carol Shaw, a former assistant to Charlie Cole and who played a leading role in the executive team, was ostracised and forced to leave the bank after her health deteriorated under the strain.

The common perception was that Allied Irish Banks allowed the dumping of the pre-1994 management team to strengthen Casey's position as chairman. (In Dublin, too, there was something of an upheaval at AIB under the new management with several senior departures.)

AIB's Dublin management team did not, however, have much influence over events at its wholly-owned Maryland acquisition. Jerry Casey resisted interference, including numerous attempts to impose AIB controls and standards throughout the bank, said an AIB insider in Dublin.

David Cronin, executive vice-president and head of treasury in Baltimore, was one of those who tried to involve Dublin more. At one stage Cronin was said to have recommended a consolidation of all of the treasury operations with AIB's treasury. Baltimore was the only location in AIB's international network of foreign currency trading desks which was not controlled and audited by AIB. He spent much of his time trying to help integrate the bank into the AIB mainstream in terms of its thinking, but his efforts were not appreciated.

For the first two years of the new leadership, the bank's performance was lacklustre. In the third quarter of 1994 First Maryland's earnings improved but bank spokesman Ron McGuirk said most of the company's income came from the sale of six branches and two other facilities in Allegany County. At the end of 1994, because of the poor numbers, no bonuses were paid to senior management. It was a significant blow to those at the top. The previous year Casey had received a $394,200 bonus on top of his $584,000 salary. That year he got no bonus, and nor did Bramble.

By February 1995 AIB chief executive, Tom Mulcahy, had conceded that profit growth in the US would be more 'modest' that year compared with the strong growth pattern in recent years, and cost control in America would be increasingly important. 'In the US, First Maryland's management team has been restructured to position the company to respond effectively to an increasingly competitive marketplace, changing customer requirements, technological advances and new product and service delivery systems,' AIB said in its group report.

The buying spree, which Jerry Casey had promised when he brought Bramble on board 'to supplement our organic growth by acquisition', was slow in coming about and the media in Ireland began to ask questions of Mulcahy. First Maryland was unable to keep up with its peers and make a significant acquisition, commented Stuart Greenberg, a private banker in Baltimore, to the *Daily Record*, Maryland's business and legal newspaper.

During 1995 the bank did consider one major acquisition. The project was discussed in great secrecy on the twenty-second floor of First Maryland headquarters. Casey and Bramble wanted AIB's backing to push ahead but the proposed acquisition was objected to by a number of senior First Maryland officials, according to an insider. They included Andrew Hiduke, David Cronin, Brian Leaney and James Smith. Brian Leaney was a highly-regarded AIB career official who had been transferred from New York to Maryland as an executive vice-president shortly after Bramble became chief executive, and Jim Smith was a senior vice-president. The officials argued that the target bank was not good enough and that First Maryland did not have the managerial depth or capacity to handle the acquisition. In the end, Casey and Bramble did not get the backing they wanted and the acquisition was aborted.

Soon afterwards Hiduke and Smith would find themselves out of the bank and Leaney, who had also apparently argued unsuccessfully for greater Dublin controls over First Maryland's operations, was transferred by Casey back to New York. Cronin was 'sent to Coventry', a colleague said. (He had also opposed Casey's takeover of York Bank in 1991 on the grounds of cost.) The episode marked a serious rift between the head of treasury and Bramble who later, citing reasons mainly to do with Cronin's competence, changed the arrangement whereby Cronin reported directly to him, requiring him to report instead to the chief finance officer, marking a disconnect between Cronin and the top echelon of the bank.

Casey and Bramble finally made a breakthrough in their search for the big prize with the acquisition of a substantial bank in neighbouring Pennsylvania.

Dauphin Deposit was based in Harrisburg in south-east Pennsylvania. Like First Maryland it had its origins in the days long before the Civil War. It was founded in 1835 as the Harrisburg Savings Institution and was the fourth-largest bank in the state, with 98 branches and 2,700 employees. It made a profit of $71 million in 1996 and had assets of $5.9 billion. It was ranked fourteenth among the country's best bank holding companies based on performance and fifth in the country for capital strength by the *US Banker*, figures too good for it to realistically expect to remain independent. Dauphin's big concern was that it would be swallowed up by a major bank like First Union or the neighbouring Pittsburgh-based Mellon Bank which would not be concerned about Dauphin's community focus. Dauphin has become 'increasingly like the pretty girl in town that hasn't married yet,' its chairman and chief executive, Chris Jennings, told the *Irish Times* Washington correspondent, Joe Carroll. The question was whether a suitor could be found that would treat her honourably.

At the end of the summer of 1996, in an unusual move, Jennings, whose role at Dauphin was said to be to 'tart her up for sale' was authorised by the Dauphin board to sound out potential partners without telling Dauphin's own investment bankers. He wrote to First Maryland in Baltimore, asking if the Irish-owned bank would be interested. By this stage AIB's Merger and Acquisitions team in the US, known as the MAC group and led by First Maryland executive vice-president Jeff Maddox had been searching for suitable acquisitions for over two years. They had their eye on Dauphin, only sixty miles north-west of Baltimore along Interstate 83 and in a region where First Maryland's small subsidiary, York Bank, had already established a foothold. They had not known if and when Dauphin would become available.

The MAC group sent AIB's business profile and earnings record to Jennings and the courtship began. It involved several meetings over sandwiches and formal dinners between Jerry Casey and Chris Jennings. The Dauphin chairman was impressed with the Cork man, describing him as 'someone who could be in the diplomatic corps.' The AIB approach, he found, was gentlemanly, 'sharp but humble', and 'deliberative to a fault'. 'Dauphin liked what it saw,' said AIB group chief executive, Tom Mulcahy.

First Maryland carried out a due diligence examination of Dauphin over a long weekend in January 1997 and submitted a bid of $1.36 billion in cash and stock. Dauphin stockholders were offered $43 in cash for their shares, 2.36 times book value. On Tuesday 21 January 1997 the Dauphin board met and agreed to the AIB terms. When they heard the news, Jennings told Joe Carroll, the bank staff in Harrisburg were 'turning cartwheels down the hall' in relief that the buyer was not a big corporate American bank.

Jennings was expecting a top position in First Maryland but that was dropped. His interview with Joe Carroll hadn't helped: it made AIB, which rigidly controlled press exposure, nervous that it could not control him, an AIB source said. If anyone was going to go on the record about the acquisition it would be Bramble, Casey or AIB chief executive, Tom Mulcahy. Jennings left with a package estimated at $6 million.

The deal added almost $6 billion in assets and 98 branches to First Maryland, giving it combined assets of $17 billion and a total of 293 branches throughout Maryland, Pennsylvania, northern Virginia and Washington DC. It increased AIB's total assets by over a third. This brought the AIB-owned bank into the big league in America: First Maryland entered the list of the top 50 banks in 45th place. It also reinstated AIB as Ireland's largest bank. Bramble said that his goal for First Maryland was to 'make this thing a regional powerhouse.'

It was a triumph for Jerry Casey. The deal was the biggest ever foreign acquisition by an Irish company. It got an enthusiastic press in the American and Irish media. In Dublin the bank's expansion was hailed as evidence of the growing strength of the Celtic Tiger. The *Irish Times* said Casey was 'the architect of AIB's strong growth in the United States.' The *Sunday Times* said that First Maryland's success could be attributed to its chairman, Jerry Casey, 'the one million pounds man who now controls just over one-third of AIB's group assets.'

Casey would in fact get compensation for 1997 of much more than a million. His total package for 1997 came to $2.67 million, including $600,000 salary, $450,000 bonus and $1.59 million in a Long-Term Incentive Plan pay-out. Similar pay-outs along with maturing stock saw Bramble's total package soar to $2.69 million and David Cronin's to over $1 million. This far outstripped the compensation for executives in Dublin. AIB, whose officials had so deeply resented the compensation paid to Charlie Cole's management team in the 1980s, defended the disparity by arguing that Casey's pay was in line with that of senior American bankers.

Under the heading, 'Allied Irish's Measured Approach to the Market Pays off Handsomely' the *American Banker* said, 'Allied Irish Banks could well be the textbook case for how a foreign banking institution can succeed in the United States.' In a reflective mood, Casey told the journal that there were two reasons for the kind of record that the Irish bank had achieved but which had eluded other foreign banks. 'We believed building market share was the single most critical element in our strategy,' he said. Secondly, AIB was careful to ensure that First Maryland would continue to run with a US culture and local management. 'Resisting the temptation to interfere can be critical,' he said, adding, 'Our main consideration will continue to be the quality of the business.' An executive who had been ousted with the Cole management team and treasured his gold quality pin said, 'I choked on my coffee when I read that.'

First Maryland's 'blue blood' team in 1980: (from left) Charles W Cole Jnr, president; Robert W Schaefer, executive vice-president; William T Murray III, executive vice-president and (seated) J Owen Cole, chairman.

Gerald B Scanlan, former AIB group chief executive and architect of the 1983 deal to take over First Maryland Bank. (*The Irish Times*)

After the deal: Charles W Cole Jnr, president of First Maryland; Patrick O'Keeffe, group chief executive of AIB; Niall Crowley, chairman of AIB and J Owen Cole, chairman of First Maryland, pictured in 1983.

Jeremiah E Casey, AIB's man in America. (*The Irish Times*)

Before the 'coup': Charles W Cole Jnr, president and CEO of First Maryland (left) with Maryland Governor William Donald Schaefer in Annapolis, 1993.

John Rusnak at the time he joined First Maryland in 1993. (*The Irish Times*)

Mathias J DeVito, president and CEO of Rouse and ally of First Maryland chairman, Jeremiah E Casey.

Walter Fatzinger Jnr, executive vice-president of First Maryland (right), with Corcoran Gallery of Art president David C Levy in 1994.

Happy together: Jeremiah E Casey, chairman, and Frank Bramble, president and CEO, after the 1994 'coup' at First Maryland.

The Rusnaks' $217,500 house in Baltimore's Mount Washington district. (*The Irish Times*)

Frank Bramble (*The Irish Times*)

AIB's former chief executive, Tom Mulcahy (right) and finance director Gary Kennedy announce profits of €609 million for the first six months of 2000. (*The Irish Times*)

A few doubts were raised, however, amid the general euphoria. The *Financial Times* questioned the wisdom of the merger, pointing out that AIB was paying nineteen times Dauphin's 1996 earnings, nearly twice the multiple at which AIB shares traded, and that forecasts of a future earnings increase were modest. It warned that AIB's growing dependence on the US markets 'could lead to underperformance'. A Chicago analyst, James Schutz, contacted by the *Harrisburg Patriot News*, said about AIB's hopes of saving $48 million annually through the consolidation, 'Quite frankly I don't know where that's going to come from.' Former First Maryland executives recalled looking at Dauphin a couple of times in the 1980s and finding its efficiency ratio was very good, meaning that there were few cost savings to be gained if they made an acquisition. 'All the excess fat had been taken out,' said one.

The Harrisburg bank had already been losing customers through high interest rates. It continued to lose market share over the next few years to the locally-managed banks Waypoint and Commerce Bank, said Tom Dochat, a reporter for the *Patriot News*. 'It was felt that they became more impersonal when a lot of the operations were transferred to Baltimore. Small businesses like to deal with people directly.'

During the fifteen-month post-merger process up to 150 people were pulled out of various sectors of the bank and sent to a 'think tank' in Hunt Valley outside Baltimore where, a participant said, we 'thought it to death'.

The operation was headed up by a new recruit to First Maryland who was also an old MNC hand. Susan Keating explained later that much necessary time was spent in upgrading both bank systems and getting staff and clients accustomed to what was going on. Some mergers were not successful because they were not effectively managed or communicated, she said.

The year after the acquisition the bank under-performed badly. In 1998 it did not meet the minimum net income established by the Management and Compensation Committee of the Board. Again no bonuses were paid. Bramble and Casey were confined to their basic salary, which was now $600,000 each.

That same year, First Maryland took a controversial decision to switch from a federally chartered bank to a state chartered bank.

Banks in the US are required to be chartered either nationally by the federal government or by the states where they have operations. Under a federal charter, a bank's records are reviewed by inspectors from the Office of the Comptroller of the Currency (OCC). This is the Washington-based regulatory body that had breathed down the necks of Bramble and his colleagues at MNC and forced them to repay their bonuses in 1990. The Office of the Comptroller of the Currency had made several inspections of First Maryland's operations, aware that the distant parent bank did not have full operational control, and had been critical of what it had found.

Though concluding that risk management of trading and deri-vatives activities was strong, the OCC raised specific concerns on several occasions about risk management in the foreign exchange trading area. It expressed concern that foreign exchange traders were exceeding limits, that there was an inadequate level of information provided to the bank's Assets and Liabilities Committee, that there was a lack of review of foreign exchange trades for off-market prices and operational and management reporting lines, and that the busi-ness reporting lines were funnelled through the head of treasury funds management, Bob Ray, instead of going independently to the top.

These critical OCC reports were not, apparently, given the atten-tion they deserved by the Baltimore bank.

With the OCC out of the picture, the bank relied on the Maryland state regulators to carry out inspections and raise warning flags about treasury risks. This placed an extraordinary burden on the office of the Maryland Commissioner of Financial Regulation. First Maryland's assets of $17 billion were almost as large as the combined assets of all sixty-six Maryland-based banks holding state charters at the time. A local businessman, Jerry Greff, opposed the switch at a public hearing on the grounds that regulators in Maryland did not have the expertise or personnel to monitor properly a bank of the size of First Maryland, but was turned down by the Bank Commissioner. Reese Nank, a spokeswoman for First Maryland said the move would save about $600,000 a year in regulatory fees and all its subsidiary banks would come under one-charter status to coincide with a new single name and corporate umbrella. The state stood to gain too, in the shape of $1.4 million in fees.

The Maryland banking regulators who would in future examine

the institution's records were ill-equipped to regulate foreign currency trading. Mary Louise Preis, Maryland's commissioner of financial regulation, spent the next year trying to hire new bank examiners to cope with the extra workload from First Maryland. In September 1999 she said her agency had taken on five new officials to augment the eight-strong staff of examiners, but that it still needed seven more. Three years later it would still be lacking nine of the twenty-three bank examiners that industry experts said it needed.

After the purchase of Dauphin Deposit, Bramble and Casey decided to get rid of the name First National Bank of Maryland, or First Maryland, which had been familiar to people in Baltimore for well over a century. A new title would be found to incorporate all First Maryland bank charters, which now included First National Bank of Maryland, Dauphin Deposit Bank of Harrisburg, York Bank of York, Pennsylvania and Omni Bank of Millsboro, Delaware.

The bank hired Interbrand Group, an international branding consultancy in New York, to help them come up with a new name. After fourteen months of market research the bank decided upon 'Allfirst Financial', with a new purple and orange logo described as a portal letting in sunlight, and a 'new day going into the new millennium.'

The transition was done 'to simplify the lives of our customers and to provide them with common product offerings, processes and technology,' Bramble told a press conference on 14 April 1999. 'Our new name better reflects who we are and who our customers and employers want us to be: a single, unified financial institution.'

But customers saw it differently. 'They ask, "Is it (the logo) a PC, a laptop, a pizza box, or a movie screen?"' admitted executive vice-president Susan Keating.

There was considerable strength of feeling against the name change among the business people of Baltimore. It was meaningless, and had none of the historical resonance of First Maryland, some felt. There was also serious attrition at Dauphin after the name was changed, with some account holders around Harrisburg signing up with other local Pennsylvania banks.

In a filing with the SEC on 16 March 2000, the bank gave another reason for changing the name. This was to incorporate the bank in Delaware where First Maryland already owned a financial centre on

60 acres of land at Mitchell Street, Millsboro which housed some of the bank's retail operations functions and which was so big that golf carts were used to get around.

'On September 15, 1999, First Maryland Bancorp ('First Maryland') was merged into Allfirst, a Delaware corporation, with Allfirst as the surviving corporation,' the filing stated. 'The purposes of the merger were to change the state of incorporation of First Maryland from Maryland to Delaware and to change the name of First Maryland to "Allfirst Financial Inc". First Maryland formed Allfirst solely for the purpose of effecting the Merger.'

The tiny maritime state next door to Maryland was a favourite location for corporations anxious to avail of its light tax regime and British-style corporate court system. Half the Fortune 500 companies of America were registered there, as were foreign companies like the Irish Press group, founded by the former Irish President, Eamon de Valera. All that was needed was a local agent.

The name-change operation meant replacing the old names on everything from high street branches to ATM cards and letterheads, and sending explanatory letters to one million customers. It cost, by the bank's reckoning, between $8 million and $12 million, but the company said it estimated expenses which had been rising by three per cent a year would shrink by two point five per cent through the consolidation.

In just over two months the name change was complete and the 'Allfirst' sign was erected on three hundred bank branches in Maryland, Delaware, southern Pennsylvania, Washington DC and northern Virginia.

Outside the bank Bramble was winning praise in his ever-expanding role as a corporate citizen. He was credited with saving the 1,600-seat Broadway-style Mechanic Theatre on Hopkins Plaza, whose stage had been graced by such stars as Katherine Hepburn and Carol Channing, and rescuing the Hippodrome Theatre, an old vaudeville hall on North Eutaw Street. First Maryland donated $500,000 to the Baltimore Centre for the Performing Arts for the construction of the Hippodrome Performing Arts Centre. He 'kept the project alive' said Richard C Mike Lewin, former secretary of Maryland's Business and Economic Development Department. Bramble served as chairman of Baltimore Centre for the Performing

Arts, the Downtown Partnership, the Greater Baltimore Committee and the University of Maryland Medical System, which would receive $1 million from the bank to fund a new emergency medical and surgical centre on Baltimore's west side. He was also on the board of Catholic Charities of the Archdiocese. His cascade of civic honours included 1995 Humanitarian of the Year from the Arthritis Foundation of Maryland, bestowed at a ceremony in the Hyatt Regency hotel, where the invocation was given by Cardinal William H Keeler.

Bonuses were restored after the bad year following the Dauphin acquisition. A contemporary edition of the *Baltimore Business Journal* drew attention to the compensation Bramble received from the bank when his salary and bonus again exceeded $1 million. 'Irish eyes are definitely smiling on Frank Bramble,' it said under the headline, 'Bramble's in the Bucks'.

In November 1998 Jerry Casey, then 58, stepped down as a member of the AIB Board and as head of its USA division. Frank Bramble was promoted to replace him as AIB director. Citing his extra workload, Bramble then relinquished the title of president.

In April 1999, Casey announced that he was retiring as chairman of Allfirst after twelve years, though he would remain a member of the Allfirst board, stay on in Baltimore and keep an office in 25 South Charles Street where he would be paid as a consultant. Bramble succeeded him, becoming chairman and chief executive. On 14 December Bramble announced that he was relinquishing the role of chief executive because of his new responsibilities as Allfirst chairman and chief executive of AIB USA, and to spend more time on acquisitions and mergers and looking for ways to exploit the Internet.

But before they could do all this, Bramble and Casey had to choose a successor to run the bank.

6

The Velvet Hammer

Who the chosen one would be was made pretty clear in an extraordinary scene staged at an invitation-only weekend retreat for bank staff at an Ocean City hotel on Maryland's Atlantic Coast in 1996. Senior executives gathered in the lobby as Frank Bramble introduced Susan Keating, the new head of retail banking, from a second-floor balcony.

'You will all love Susan Keating,' he cried to the upturned faces, according to the *Baltimore Sun*. 'You will all love Susan Keating.'

Keating had arrived in the bank as yet another former colleague of Bramble's from MNC. A native of Los Angeles she had a 1972 degree in arts and sciences from Chicago's Northwestern University and worked briefly as a high school English teacher before starting her banking career. She thought about being a journalist but she credited her grandfather with persuading her that she had the acumen to do well in the business world. In 1974 she became the first woman to be accepted for Milwaukee First Bank System's management training programme. 'They took a risk with me and it worked out well,' she said later. Her friends were surprised at her move to banking which they considered very 'traditional', with long hours. She rose to the position of senior manager of retail and marketing in Milwaukee and in 1988 was recruited by MNC in Baltimore as head of consumer banking. There she advanced to executive vice-president under Frank Bramble, with responsibility for overseeing the day-to-day running of the bank.

Keating stayed with MNC after the failing institution was taken over in October 1993 by NationsBank. She was soon afterwards appointed president of NationsBank Maryland. She ran NationsBank Maryland's operations and its consumer banking affairs for the mid-Atlantic region.

She then got a new boss, R Eugene Taylor, former president of NationsBank Florida who was made president of NationsBank mid-

Atlantic banking group after the MNC takeover. The two bankers' personalities were utterly different and conflict was inevitable. Susan Keating had a reputation for being very cautious in reaching decisions, rarely raising her voice and preferring to achieve consensus before making a move. Taylor once boasted about himself: 'I'm short. I'm abrupt. I don't like being told I can't do something. I don't have a great deal of patience.'

Stories appeared in the Baltimore media about open hostility between the two, with Taylor 'blasting her out' in front of colleagues. 'He would really lose it in her presence,' a banker told Bill Atkinson of the *Baltimore Sun*. 'He got pretty loud. It was really ugly. Not a pretty sight.'

Taylor, a marathon runner, ran the bank in the management style imposed by its chairman, a former US marine called Hugh L McColl, who kept a hand grenade on his desk and favoured staff meetings where executives whipped up fervour with impassioned speeches.

The personality problems were exacerbated by disagreements about how the bank should be run. Keating's heavy outside schedule was also apparently an issue. Keating had joined Maryland Governor, Parris N Glendening's 21-member Economic Development Commission and the board of Empower Baltimore! which oversaw a $100 million federal grant for the city. Her civic contacts helped bring in millions of dollars worth of business and made her popular with city and state officials. James T Brady, Maryland's secretary of Business and Economic Development, described himself as a 'huge fan' of Keating for her 'key role' in developing the state's economic policy. She belonged to so many boards and was in such demand that a public relations assistant had to screen requests at her office.

Her public status was further enhanced when in 1994 she was named one of the 'Magnificent Seven' by *Business and Professional Women/USA*. But it wasn't enough to preserve her job.

'What Susan Keating and Frank Bramble were faced with was the fact that McColl had sent in an enforcer to get rid of them after the merger of NationsBank with MNC,' said a former executive vice-president at First Maryland. 'That was how he did it. Taylor was the enforcer. Sometimes the enforcer would arrive from headquarters, take the CEO out to coffee, tell him he was fired, and then take a plane back.'

At the end of June 1995 Taylor, acting as enforcer for McColl, placed Keating on administrative leave over what were termed 'differences in management philosophy.' NationsBank said that Taylor had taken over her responsibilities. A NationsBank board member told the *Baltimore Sun* that her departure was precipitated by an offer of a senior job at First Maryland, which she could not accept immediately because of the terms of her contract with NationsBank.

Some time later, Susan Keating reappeared in her NationsBank office. Taylor reportedly confronted her as she met with colleagues. 'What are you doing here? You are on administrative leave,' he said. She replied simply: 'I'm back.' 'We have to talk, right now,' Taylor retorted. After their talk, Keating left the bank for good. It was early August 1995. For the first time in her banking career she was out of work.

Keating's spell of unemployment lasted for several months, until Frank Bramble brought her to First Maryland as head of retail banking early in 1996. Bramble and Casey announced the appointment to key managers in an internal memo which also said there would be yet another shake-up in senior management. 'Susan Keating joins our company today as executive vice-president and leader of retail banking,' the memo said. 'Susan brings to our company a wealth of retail banking experience with a number of prominent banking companies.'

The memo added that joining Susan in retail banking would be Andrew Hiduke. This was seen as a demotion for the human resources director who had written the highly-critical memo to Frank Bramble about staff morale more than a year earlier. Hiduke would leave the bank the following year. Brian King, Jerry Casey's loyal ally, was made head of the human resources division and promoted to executive vice-president.

Promotion for Keating came rapidly. On 8 July 1997, the day First Maryland finalised its acquisition of Dauphin, she was made president and chief executive of the Harrisburg-based bank, replacing long-standing Dauphin boss, Christopher R Jennings. She moved house with her husband, John, an executive of the MBNA credit card company, and their daughter to Pennsylvania to be near her new office. Within eighteen months she was elevated in the ranks again when Frank Bramble was promoted to head of AIB's USA division and stepped down as president of Allfirst. He named Keating as president and chief operating officer of the bank, effective from 11 January 1999.

'She's an outstanding manager and did a great job managing and growing our Pennsylvania franchise,' said Bramble, adding that the board 'thinks Susan one of the most talented banking executives in the US.' She was someone 'who keeps the oars moving in the same direction.'

Perhaps mindful of her treatment at the hands of Taylor in NationsBank, Susan Keating showed that she too could be tough in dealing with a rival. Keating's main competitor for the job of president had been executive vice-president Walter R Fatzinger, head of First Maryland's Greater Washington region and also one of the MNC people brought in by Bramble. Known affectionately as 'Fats', he was highly respected by both the old and new guard as a 'first-class operator'. Insiders said he had also been promised that if Keating was promoted he would not have to report to her. By one account, just after Susan Keating's promotion had been announced, she called him at his desk in Baltimore from her office in Harrisburg in Pennsylvania. She wanted to see him, right then, in her office. Faced with the choice of dropping everything and driving sixty miles, or saying something rude and quitting, he chose the latter, according to a close colleague. Fatzinger, 56, retired as soon as Susan took over as president. It was the start of a new round of retirements and firings.

Senior vice-president, Thomas Fitzsimmons, Bramble's brother-in-law, who had been given the information technology brief by Bramble, was promoted to executive vice-president when Keating became president. He, too, was soon to depart in equally dramatic circumstances. When he told Keating that he was leaving (he did not want to report to her), she had him escorted out of the bank by the head of security.

Executive vice-president and former acquisitions head, Jeff Maddox, considered by staff to be like a son to Frank Bramble, also left when Keating became president. Richard H White was another to go at this time. After spending his entire career in international banking and loan review, White had been transferred in the Bramble reshuffle of January 1996 to head up Omni Bank, the revitalised credit card division of First Maryland. White got the message, quit and found a new vocation as a church minister. 'Frank and Susan, they eat their young,' quipped a former vice-president.

In December 1999 Keating made it all the way to the top. She was appointed chief executive officer to succeed Bramble. At 49 she became one of the youngest women bank chief executives in the United States. She welcomed the opportunity, she said, 'to take the company to the next level.'

The staff changes continued apace. Altogether up to twenty vice-presidents and top executives – many of them brought in by Bramble from MNC – would leave Allfirst for various reasons, among them constant reorganisation, exasperation with a style of management which involved meeting after meeting, and a feeling that Keating was not experienced enough to be chief executive. (One very senior bank executive left soon after being caught on security cameras having sex with a junior colleague in the bank's underground car park. The video was seen by fascinated co-workers.)

One senior vice-president who departed was 43-year-old Jennifer Lambdin, president and chief investment officer of Allied Investment Advisors, the bank's investment arm, and a veteran of First Maryland who had been protected by Fatzinger for her investment skills. Well-liked by staff and senior management her investment performance had been strong and senior colleagues tried to make her stay. Despite her twenty-five years in investment management, and her record of increasing the assets under management as president of the bank's Allied Investment Advisors division from $4 billion to $15 billion in four years, Keating asked Lambdin to take on retail banking. She left and went back to work for Charlie Cole who was on his way to becoming chairman and chief executive of Legg Mason Trust, situated in the next downtown block. Judy McCoy and Ron Perrone, former managing directors with Allied Investment Advisors, also left.

Diane E Murphy, the highly-respected head of human resources and also a First Maryland veteran, went to pursue other interests in November 1999, reportedly because she did not wish to further endure the crude verbal behaviour of an MNC import, who also eventually left the bank after complaints about his actions. The number three man at the bank, vice-chairman, Jerome W Evans, who was brought by Bramble from MNC and promoted to vice-chairman when Keating became president, and who was one of only three executives still reporting directly to Bramble, took early retirement in May 2000.

The list of departures also included Charles G Cusic Jr, the former president of Allfirst Trust, and Steven M Levine, a veteran of fifteen years with First Maryland, who left his position as senior vice-president to take a job as president of a real estate company, and vice-presidents Denise Stokes and Bonnie Stern.

Keating got the nickname inside the bank of 'the Velvet Hammer' for her way of getting rid of people. 'She liked that,' said a former colleague.

The effect of all the changes was that a feeling grew that the two people running the bank did not have the expertise, basic knowledge and leadership skills to attract and keep people, and a multiplicity of problems arose from 'putting people in the wrong pew'. There was a tradition in the Irish bank to rotate. In the United States that did not work so well and in Allfirst senior executives were put in charge of speciality sections about which they knew little.

Brian King was a case in point. Jerry Casey's confidante was made compliance officer and given auditing and risk management on top of human resources, but his whole experience had been in personnel.

Keating had a reputation for being very bright but for being a micro-manager with a penchant for red tape. One of her critics in AIB conceded that she was 'very energetic, very personable and warm, very courteous, able to make a great presentation. She talked a great game.' She was very focussed on the details of public relations. She was reported to personally amend dozens of drafts of a news release. Keating once went through about fifty photographs of herself before selecting one for use in a marketing promotion, according to the *Baltimore Sun*. A reporter from that newspaper who made a passing reference in an article to her career as a schoolteacher was informed sharply that that she was not pleased, as it was not relevant to her banking career.

Critics said ideas languished at endless meetings that she chaired. Regular sessions in the 'Office of the President', known by its acronym as the 'OOPS' meetings, went on for a long time, with department heads surreptitiously reading newspapers. But she could be tough and determined when she wanted.

Keating also brought some of her own people into the bank, including a former college room-mate from Minneapolis whom she appointed executive vice-president and head of human resources in early 2000. Taylor Foss had been senior vice-president of human resources at First Bank, now US Bank, in Minneapolis. She came to an arrangement with Keating that allowed her to continue living in Minneapolis, over 1,000 miles away, and to commute to Baltimore at the start of every week, and return home on Thursday evenings and work Friday at home. In Baltimore during the week she stayed at the exclusive Harbour Court Hotel. Her dog accompanied her on these flights back and forward across the United States. The expense and time spent in transit to and from a faraway city by the executive responsible for the 6,000 bank staff living in the mid-Atlantic area was the subject of much critical comment in and outside the bank. The *Minneapolis Star* reported in August 2001, in an article about a group of business women known as 'Synnikan', of which Taylor Foss was a member, that she 'travels weekly (amassing frequent-flier mileage) with her dog to Baltimore, where she is executive vice-president of Allfirst Bank.'

Keating's civic activities multiplied, frequently taking her away from the twenty-second floor. She served as a board member for the Financial Services Roundtable on which she chaired the Consumer Issues Committee, for the Baltimore Symphony Orchestra, the Greater Baltimore Committee, the Baltimore Life Insurance Companies, Empower Baltimore Management Corporation, the Maryland Business Council, Union Memorial Hospital, the University of Maryland's Shock Trauma Center, the Baltimore Museum of Art, St. Paul's School for Girls, the B&O Railroad Museum, and the Fannie Mae National Advisory Council. She was also a trustee of the York College of Pennsylvania. She co-chaired the Governor's Economic Development Policy Committee in Maryland and was Banking Chair for the US Savings Bond National Volunteer Committee. She was a member of the Council of One Hundred, a select group of professional women graduates of Northwestern University and was selected as one of the top 100 Professional Women in Maryland and one of Pennsylvania's 50 Best Women.

Shortly after becoming president of Allfirst in 1999, Keating declared that the AIB-owned bank was entering a growth phase. But it was not performing up to the high expectations raised by the purchase of Dauphin and there were no more bank buy-outs on the horizon. The Pennsylvania acquisition had failed to boost earnings as much as anticipated and the Allfirst operation was being scrutinised more heavily in Dublin as AIB's Irish and UK operations outshone the US performance.

After taking over Dauphin, Allfirst's core momentum began to slow for the first time in many years, said NCB Stockbrokers in Dublin in a report in February 2002. 'Revenue slowed following the deal and has never really picked up since.' Net income reached a high point of $205.9 million in 1998 but dropped back. During the fastest economic expansion in the United States on record, from 1997 to 2000, Allfirst fell behind similar-sized banks in three out of four years based on its return on assets, the key ratio for measuring bank profitability, according to a separate report from SNL Securities.

Though accounting for little more than 30 per cent of AIB assets Keating was earning almost as much as the CEO of the parent organisation. She received $600,000 in salary and $336,000 in bonus in 2000, totalling $936,000. By comparison AIB's chief executive in 2000, Tom Mulcahy received €1.2 million in compensation, worth $1.076 million.

With the bank under-performing, the pressure to pare back costs and to improve performance became intense. 'If you sat at a budget meeting or before the CFO [Chief Financial Officer] for a review and said that sales were less than the prior year, that just wasn't acceptable. You just had to find a way to find increases,' a former senior executive told the *Baltimore Sun*, adding that the pressure to make the numbers came from AIB as well as from within.

'I think these criticisms are inappropriate and misplaced,' said Susan Keating in response to a scathing *Baltimore Sun* article about her style of leadership and stewardship of the bank. 'My leadership and performance speak for itself [sic].' At a Baltimore function for top women she accused Jennifer Lambdin of leaking stories about her to the media, which Lambdin denied.

In January 2002, Susan Keating was appointed to the nine-member AIB group executive committee chaired by AIB chief executive Michael Buckley. She was the first woman to be appointed to such a key top job in Irish banking. She had become not just one of the leading women bankers in the United States, but the leading woman in Irish banking.

The risk consequences of years of resistance to AIB controls at Allfirst, and cost cutting in every department did not, however, go unnoticed in other quarters in Dublin. On 1 June 2001 a flyer was circulated by a group of dissident shareholders citing AIB's problems managing its subsidiaries. It said: 'There is a mathematical certainty that a financial asteroid is on a collision course with Allied Irish Banks, probably from Poland, the USA or the capital markets.'

7

The Home Office Spy

There was one person amongst the ranks of Allfirst senior managers whom Susan Keating could not move around or fire. This was David Cronin, an executive vice-president and head of the bank's treasury department. The tall, witty Cork man was put there by AIB in 1989 to run the treasury and keep an eye on the flow of money for Dublin. It was believed that Cronin's presence in Baltimore would give AIB comfort that the treasury was in capable hands.

Apart from Jerry Casey and a few junior officials, David Cronin was the only Irish person posted to the bank. The Baltimore management controlled Cronin's treasury budget, his salary and his bonus, but Cronin's job was basically to apply AIB policy to the treasury operation. Dublin believed it had a stronger treasury than First Maryland, and that with Cronin there AIB would have a good point man to monitor its American subsidiary.

Cronin was a former Irish Central Bank employee who at one time managed an AIB trading operation consisting of some forty to fifty traders, including currency traders. As a veteran of AIB's inner circle, he consulted frequently with a network of highly placed former colleagues in Dublin. As chairman of the American bank's key Asset and Liability Committee (ALCO), and a member of AIB's group-wide ALCO and its Market Strategy Committee, he was in a unique position to report back and forth.

Cronin's files and telephone records showed that he kept up a constant chatter with AIB executives in Dublin, particularly AIB group treasurer, Pat Ryan. Cronin would discuss any significant policy or strategic matter with Ryan before getting formal approval from Bramble or Keating.

Cronin said he felt that at the beginning he was treated as the 'home office spy'. American colleagues recall that at first he was largely excluded from senior management meetings and interactions. 'Initially there was definitely the impression that he was a spy,' said a former executive, 'but David really grew on people and he would go on golf trips and he was good fun.' He was a bigger social hit at the bank than the reserved Jerry Casey. 'He was not highly skilled in securities but we found him a very nice person, likeable, with a wonderful sense of humour.' He and his wife, Karen, became popular guests at dinner parties in Washington where senior American politicians and prominent Irish diplomats attended.

One other official working in treasury was also an Irish expatriate, and extremely popular with American colleagues. Joe O'Sullivan was such a hit, in fact, that in the traders' favourite watering hole, Peter's Pour House in Water Street, a brass plaque with the date 1986 – 1998 was erected on a wooden bar pillar with the engraved tribute: 'Joe O'Sullivan drank here. Ní Fheicfimíd A Leithéad Arís (We shall not see his like again)'.

Cronin took up residence with his family in a beautiful house with a long winding driveway in the wooded Baltimore neighbourhood of Ruxton Riderwood. He joined the boards of the Baltimore Chapter of the Boy Scouts of America and the Shrine of the Sacred Heart School. He became well known to his neighbours as an active member of the community.

The foreign currency section of the treasury was a very minor part of bank operations when Cronin took over, though he inherited an expensive problem with the US Treasury. A branch office manager had failed to file reports on one hundred and eleven currency transactions of more than $10,000 each by three companies between 1987 and 1989, as required by the Bank Secrecy Act, a US law designed to prevent money laundering. Bank officials pleaded that the branch manager had simply misinterpreted the rules. Nevertheless the US Treasury Department fined the bank $950,000 in a ruling issued in March 1992. Assistant Secretary of the US Treasury, Peter Nunez, warned that such a substantial penalty 'will send a strong message to financial institutions' not to break the law. The penalty was eventually reduced to $400,000 and a 'slap on the wrist'.

The episode underlined another big difference between Irish and American banking cultures. In Ireland if there was a technical breach of the regulations – and banks ran into them all the time – it could be sorted out quickly, but in the United States the attitude was always that anyone skimping a regulation was in violation, and had to face the consequences.

There was no proprietary trading – betting the bank's money against foreign currency movements to make a profit – at the bank in those days. The First Maryland currency traders only handled foreign currency exchange for clients. 'We would never have gone off betting the dollar against the yen,' said a former senior First Maryland executive. 'We weren't Citicorp. It didn't make any sense.'

From his arrival in Baltimore in 1989, Cronin reported directly to the CEO, but Bramble, who had no treasury experience and who had clashed with Cronin over acquisitions policy, changed the arrangement, asking him to report instead to the chief financial officer, Jerome W Evans, the former MNC executive vice-president with responsibility for overseeing the treasury. Evans left the bank in May 2000, six months after Keating took over as chief executive. AIB management made it clear that they wanted to resume the old arrangement of Cronin reporting to the chief executive, to help Keating understand treasury operations.

Under Keating's management, the bank was without a full-time chief financial officer for ten months. In March 2001 Maurice Crowley arrived from AIB to take up the vacancy. This was widely seen as an attempt by Ballsbridge to assert more control over AIB's subsidiary. Crowley came from one of Ireland's top banking families; his father was the late AIB chairman, Niall Crowley, and his uncle was the Bank of Ireland governor, Laurence Crowley. He was a chartered accountant with experience in venture capital markets, strategic planning, electronic banking and investor relations, and had worked in the US in the early 1980s as an audit manager with KPMG, but he had no direct experience of treasury operations. His role was also to assist with geographical expansion and other acquisition plans.

Foreign exchange speculation was not meant to be part of the core business of Allfirst, a retail bank that focussed on individual and business loans through its branches, and on its trust business. In terms of formal risk limits, the proprietary trading operation introduced by Cronin in 1990 was very small, and the value-at-risk limit for all foreign exchange trading was never more than $2.5 million.

The proprietary trader had a monthly stop-loss limit of only $200,000 – if his losses exceeded $200,000 he would have to stop trading for the rest of that month. The budgeted annual revenue for all foreign exchange trading ran to between $1 million and $2 million.

Susan Keating did not mention concerns about risks in the foreign currency trading operation when she gave an extensive interview to the *Journal of Lending and Credit Risk Management* in May 2000. Asked what she thought 'the biggest risks on the horizon' were for Allfirst, she replied that some things worried her more than others: there was 'great risk in the amount of change bankers were dealing with – technological, economic and the competitive environment.' Employees must be thoroughly trained, she said. At Allfirst they stuck to the business they knew, 'limiting business in areas we consider riskier.'

When David Cronin took over the Treasury in First Maryland in 1989, the bank's day-to-day trading activities were chiefly characterised by straightforward buying and selling of currencies on behalf of clients. The bank had big corporate clients, such as toolmaker Black & Decker, which did international business and worked through foreign currencies.

In 1990, however, Cronin appointed a trader to use First Maryland treasury funds to speculate a little on the currency markets to turn a profit. That trader largely used 'directional' spot and forward trading, i.e. he made simple bets that particular currencies would rise and fall. A spot trade is an exchange of two currencies with a two-day time frame at a fixed, agreed-upon exchange rate. (Buy a bar of chocolate for cash and you've done a spot trade, usually settling in ten seconds; agree a price to buy it next week and you've done a forward trade.) A forward trade is an exchange of currencies with a settlement date more than two days after the trade date, typically within a few months after the trade date.

The trader left the bank in 1993 and Cronin asked Robert Ray, a senior vice-president in the First Maryland treasury, and a long-time bank employee generally considered to be knowledgeable about the financial markets, to find a replacement. A friend of Ray's at First Fidelity Bank in Philadelphia recommended a former colleague who had worked there called John Rusnak.

Bob Ray and David Cronin invited Rusnak for an interview. They asked him about his expertise. Rusnak said he could use more sophisticated methods than the outgoing trader to swell First

Maryland's treasury profits. He could engage in option trades. These involved buying and selling an opportunity to enter into a future foreign exchange spot trade at an agreed-upon exchange rate known as the 'strike price'. The buyer paid a cash premium to the seller to acquire the right – but not the obligation – to exchange currency at an agreed-upon price at a future date known as the 'expiration date'. The buyer was, however, not required to exercise the option, which was essentially a form of insurance to offset losses when the currency markets moved in the opposite direction to the trader's bet. Their use was known as hedging and they were a standard way of reducing the risks involved in currency trading.

Rusnak claimed that he could consistently make more money by running a large option book hedged in the cash markets, buying options when they were cheap and selling them when they were expensive. Cronin and Ray were intrigued. Cronin felt there was money to be made in his department. Foreign exchange trading at AIB in Dublin, where his own experience had been, regularly made a significant profit. Running a real 'forex' outpost at First Maryland would give him a quasi-independent role – almost a separate AIB operation – at a bank where the chairman and chief executive gave him the cold shoulder.

Rusnak got the job, starting in July 1993.

John Rusnak was born in Pennsylvania, and raised as a Catholic in a one-storey house in Bristol Township, a tidy working-class suburb of Philadelphia. His father, Emil, was a retired steel worker and his mother, Angelina, registered death certificates for the state. He was brighter than the average kids at Harry S Truman High School in Philadelphia and on graduation was accepted by Bucknell University in Lewisburg, Pennsylvania. There he continued to shine, twice making the Dean's list. He is remembered by Edward Robinson, who was the president of Rusnak's college class, as a 'quiet but active kid,' who 'navigated the institution and his fellow students seamlessly.'

After gaining a degree in economics in 1986, he got a job as a currency options trader at the First Fidelity Bank in Philadelphia. Two years later Rusnak moved to New York to do the same thing at Chemical Bank, a predecessor of JP Morgan Chase. A former Chemical Bank colleague said he was 'a nice guy, good at what he did.' He married and settled down with his wife, Linda, in Westport, Connecticut, within commuting distance of the city. But he was unhappy with the pressure at Chemical Bank. By 1993 he was ready to leave and seek work elsewhere when Ray and Cronin offered him the job.

John and Linda Rusnak sold their house in Connecticut for $375,000 and moved to Baltimore. After looking at several properties in the north-western suburbs, the couple decided on a Victorian frame house on the 6000 block of Smith Avenue in the Mount Washington district. The rambling old hillside house, with wrap-around balcony and carriage house, partly obscured by pine trees, was within walking distance of a Catholic church and school. The neighbours included Baltimore's chief of police and several lawyers. They bought the three-storey building for $217,500 after a bit of hard bargaining with the owner, Samuel Dell. The couple financed the deal with a mortgage of $135,000 from Harbour Federal Savings.

The house was in a shambles. It had been occupied for many years by a disabled woman who installed special devices all over the house to move around, and had partitioned off the eight bedrooms into three apartments and four kitchens. Rusnak would be kept busy in his spare time knocking down false walls and 'getting a lot of fun' fixing it up. He liked to tell the story of how Linda had wielded a sledgehammer during the renovations. Soon it was a fine house again, painted a shade of magnolia with green shutters.

Rusnak settled into a routine at the bank, arriving every morning around 7.00 am to work in a beige-coloured cubicle on the twelfth floor of the bank's headquarters building, dressed in typical trader's gear of khaki trousers and buttoned-down Oxford shirt with no tie, and leaving after 4.00 pm when the US markets closed.

The following year, 1994, officials from AIB group internal audit in Dublin undertook a review of the treasury operation in Baltimore at Cronin's suggestion. It was the only time that the AIB auditors, with their vast experience in assessing risk in AIB's big Dublin foreign currency trading operation, did a check of the Baltimore treasury until January 2002. They now knew about Rusnak's risky operation, but did not have a 'mandate' to audit any of First Maryland's business under the 'light hand' approach to its US subsidiary. AIB's group treasurer only set the limits for Rusnak's trading and that of another trader who did foreign currency transactions for bank clients.

There was resistance at the Baltimore bank to anything other than minimal oversight by AIB over bank controls. 'Pat Ryan, the group treasurer, was not empowered to apply fully the market risk standards to Allfirst [First Maryland],' an insider said. 'The Group Credit Risk was only permitted a minimal role of inquiry at Allfirst, and the Operational Risk Management was not allowed near Allfirst. Eugene McErlean, AIB group internal auditor, despite his title, had no influence over Allfirst and his experienced treasury audit teams used in Dublin and London could not be sent to examine Allfirst, which was left pitifully exposed. A third of the group balance sheet was exempted from these central controls which shareholders were led to believe applied across all the businesses of the group.'

A former AIB head of internal audit, Tony Spollen, who highlighted the bank's liability for unpaid DIRT tax, proposed a few years earlier that his division should be allowed to audit Allfirst. He got nowhere. His relationship with the bank's chief executive at the time, Gerry Scanlan, was extremely poor, (he retired shortly after AIB rejected his DIRT tax conclusions), suggesting that any proposals he made would not be well received by management.

In 1995, the Baltimore bank's own efficiency sub-committee raised doubts about Rusnak's activity, and suggested the possibility of eliminating or scaling back proprietary trading. Big institutions in New York or Hong Kong would employ proprietary traders to use the bank's cash to make money, but the profit margins were exceptionally thin, and having one dealer in a bank the size of First Maryland did not make sense.

Cronin spoke to his colleagues in Dublin and explained that his plan was to have a 'niche' currency player in Baltimore. In the end Cronin apparently decided to scale back the amount of directional proprietary trading to satisfy concerns but, as Eugene Ludwig would later note in his report, he did not scale back Rusnak's use of options and futures in proprietary trading.

For most of the first four years, however, everything went well. Rusnak delivered as promised. Despite the planned scaling back of directional trading, it was what he mostly did, making simple bets that the market would move in a particular direction, and only occasionally engaging in complex option transactions. He appeared extremely confident about what he was doing, even cocky, and liked to show off his skills. Once, in late-1997, a business reporter, Bill Atkinson, was admitted to the cavernous twelfth-floor trading room in First Maryland to watch John Rusnak and his colleague, Matthew F Kozak, vice-president of foreign exchange, at work at the currency trading desk. The reporter was researching an article on international currency speculation prompted by the Asian economic crisis. He described the scene in the *Baltimore Sun*:

> The two traders had their eyes trained on a bank of computers. Rusnak slid his chair behind a computer called the Electronic Brokering System, which showed the prices that currency traders around the world were willing to pay to exchange dollars for marks, francs, pounds and other currencies.
>
> 'Wait a minute,' Rusnak said. He punched the keyboard and in an instant exchanged $5 million for DM8.6 million with New York's Chase Manhattan Bank. In seconds the value of the dollar fell and Rusnak struck, buying back the $5 million he sold for a quick profit.
>
> 'If we could do that every time we would be sitting in our bathrobes smoking a pipe,' said Kozak.

8

Fake Docs

But John Rusnak couldn't do it every time. In fact more often than not Rusnak was not making a quick profit but a quick loss. He bet wrongly and often that the Japanese yen would increase in value against the US dollar, and bought a great deal of yen for future delivery, only to see the value of his forward positions decline. He made one-way bets, failing to hedge them with a reverse option contract.

It was the most fundamental mistake for a trader to make. It is common in American banks for traders to be fired if they do not show regular profits and Rusnak feared that if he lost $1 million by the end of the year his desk would be closed down.

That was when the fraud started.

As the losses accumulated, Rusnak found a way to hide them. He invented bogus trades. He created fictitious options in the bank's system to make it look as if his real positions were hedged. In *Rogue Trader*, his account of the Barings Bank scandal, Nick Leeson described the agonising hours he spent with a scissors, a stick of paste and a fax machine to create a false £50 million confirmation document to keep the bank's auditors off his back.

When Rusnak required confirmations from counterparties to validate his trades, he simply manufactured the documents on his personal computer, in a file which at some point he named 'fake docs', and printed them out. This file would expand over the next five years to include a wide range of documents, complete with fake logos, purporting to come from financial institutions in the United States and throughout Asia. All he had to do was click on the file and print off letters or telefaxes as required.

In any other bank Rusnak would not have been able to get away with it. Every time Rusnak entered a trade involving a cash transaction in the bank's Opics and Devon system, which was used to record daily, weekly, monthly and annual profit and loss records for each trader, another treasury employee was supposed to check it in the 'back office'. The back office was deliberately located in another part of the building to prevent collusion. A designated back office employee was supposed to confirm the existence and purpose of the trade from the back office of the counterparty bank. In modern banks where foreign exchange is traded, confirmations are automatically sought and received electronically within minutes. The back office employees in Baltimore relied on old-fashioned fax or mail confirmations, and, incredibly, were prepared to accept these from the trader himself.

Rusnak had to ensure that none of the bank's other checks and control systems would expose his deceit. He found a way to get the bogus options onto the bank's books. At the end of each session he would routinely enter the day's dealing transactions into the trading system. Among these would be two bogus trades entered simultaneously. For example, one would be an option sold to a bank in Tokyo or Singapore to sell yen at a specified price in the future. The other would be an offsetting option from the same financial institution, to buy the Japanese currency at a specified price in the future. The two options would offset each other. He made it appear as though both of the option contracts carried an identical premium in the same currency. This way he would ensure that the back office staff would not have to make a payment on behalf of First Maryland to the counter-party, so no questions were raised. The two payments would simply cancel each other out.

There was, however, one significant difference. The option involving the receipt of the premium would expire on the same day it was purportedly written, but the other option would expire weeks later, typically in a month or so. Thus the liability represented by the one-day bogus option would not appear on the books, but the unexpired deep-in-the-money option for which the bank had supposedly paid a huge premium would appear as an asset.

This was nonsensical to anyone examining the trades. The different expiration dates should mean different premium amounts. But nobody in treasury noticed anything out of the ordinary. The treasury staff did not prepare any reports listing the expiring one-day options. The system did not automatically alert supervisors if such options were not exercised. And the back office accepted the bogus confirmations that Rusnak provided rather than verifying them independently.

Then Rusnak began to trade larger amounts to try to get out of his losses.

Sometime in 1997 AIB was made aware of the extraordinary levels Rusnak's trading had reached. A manager of AIB's Strategic Asset and Liability Management Committee who reported to group treasurer, Pat Ryan, showed that he knew at that time that the bank's average foreign exchange option book was '$1 billion nominal' and that 'John Rusneck (sic)', the foreign exchange options dealer, was accountable for 95 per cent of the bank's foreign exchange risk with about 100 transactions a day, of which 80 per cent were speculative.

That year Rusnak did not show results. Indeed he did not even merit a bonus on top of his $102,000 salary. To traders the salary is often not as important as the end-of-the-year bonus, and not to get one is a mark of a very bad year. Rusnak was entitled to a bonus equal to 30 per cent of any net trading profits he generated in excess of five times his salary. So his net trading profits, if any, were less than $510,000 that year. Not only did he not merit a bonus in 1997, but Rusnak secretly ran up losses totalling $29.1 million.

For most of the following year Rusnak continued to lose money through making bad bets on the yen and continued entering pairs of bogus trades into the system and printing fake confirmation documents for the back office.

In September 1998 Rusnak found that he no longer needed to run off the bogus confirmations for option contracts that cancelled each other out. He apparently persuaded the treasury's operations and financial analyst, Lawrence Smith, who was responsible for examining the daily journal and preparing a list of brokers and financial institutions to contact to verify all trades, that there was no need for confirmations of his matching option contracts as there was no net transfer of cash. This perhaps suited the back office staff member, suggested Ludwig later, as confirming the options by telephone with Singapore and Hong Kong banks would mean working through the night because of the time difference.

From his experience at the trading desk in Chemical Bank, Rusnak knew that the controls at the Baltimore bank were full of holes. Verifying a currency dealer's trades by telephone or fax was an archaic system long-since abandoned by the major international financial institutions in the United States and by AIB's treasury in Dublin. Currency transactions entered into by AIB traders were automatically confirmed with the counterparty within a couple of minutes through the Crossmar Matching System used by about a thousand banks, corporations and fund management companies. This was an automated system supplied by Crossmar, a subsidiary of Citigroup, for matching foreign exchange and securities trades. If the details of a transaction entered into by two parties do not match, both were instantly notified.

AIB had software that would effectively track and control the actions of its traders in any of its offices around the world but, crucially, only a portion of that system had been implemented in Baltimore. With only two employees on the currency trading desk, neither bank apparently considered the expense of fully integrating this control system to be justified.

However, it wasn't just the bogus trades or confirmations that the treasury failed to independently confirm. In 1998 the bank's internal audit criticised the treasury for not obtaining monthly foreign exchange prices independently of the trader, as required by the bank's fund management policy. This was a concern that had been raised by the federal regulators, the Office of the Comptroller of the Currency, three years earlier. The OCC had also raised concerns, largely ignored by Allfirst, about Rusnak exceeding his limits, about the inadequate level of information about foreign exchange dealing to the banks Assets and Liabilities Committee (ALCO), chaired by Cronin, and about the fact that operational, management and business reporting lines funnelled into Bob Ray.

Bob Ray was considered pretty savvy about the financial markets. Cronin placed a high degree of trust in him. Ray often used his strong personality to defend Rusnak when rows broke out between the front and the back office. While reportedly hard on his subordinates – he did not tolerate people he believed incompetent – Ray strongly defended Rusnak when the back office or risk assessment personnel raised any queries about his trading. He regarded his protégé as a star trader with the potential to generate revenues of millions of dollars. More than once he chided Rusnak for his behaviour towards the back office, but in his performance evaluation he praised Rusnak's teamwork and interpersonal skills.

The controls were so lax that Rusnak found that he could act with more and more impunity. Sometimes he 'borrowed' overnight a sum like $10 million out of the treasury desk and called it carrying costs, and he would then return it next morning while he entered the $10 million as interest on his trading account.

The upshot of Rusnak's flow of 'fake docs' was that he was able to create at will assets on the bank's books without ever having to pay for them, and these assets concealed the losses in his spot wagers on the yen against the dollar. He did it day after day, keeping the non-existent asset on the books by repeatedly rolling it over into new bogus options as the old ones became due.

At the end of 1998 he fared better in terms of compensation. His net trading profit for the bank was estimated at $1.068 million. Rusnak brought home a bonus of $128,102 on top of his salary of $104,000.

But Rusnak's hidden losses had also gone up. He had now secretly gambled away $41.5 million of the bank's money and more daring means would have to be used to try to get it back.

9

Inelegant Fraud

The strain of hiding his growing losses showed in Rusnak's character at work. He exhibited an unpleasant temper and displayed bullying behaviour towards colleagues. Staff in the back office found him arrogant and abusive. A show of intimidation of back office staff might, of course, keep them from looking too closely at what he was doing. David Cronin and Bob Ray defended Rusnak when storms blew up and they tolerated the friction between the trader and the back office staff. Cronin believed that John Rusnak was fundamentally a good person. Maurice Crowley went with Rusnak to a football game and found him to be a bit cocky but a regular guy.

Rusnak admitted to a friend that he was two totally separate people. At work he was more aggressive. He pushed people around and he didn't keep regular hours. He would golf all day, go to lunch and not come back. He admitted that the way he treated people wasn't right.

Outside the bank Rusnak was different. People knew him as a nice guy. He was conducting a different life outside work: around his family, the church and voluntary work. When he dropped into Peter's Pour House on Water Street near bank headquarters, Rusnak would quietly sip his drinks, rarely downing more than three bottles of Heineken. He usually hung around the edge of the crowd. He was not at all like Joe O'Sullivan, the Irish trader commemorated on a brass plaque in the bar, who was always a lot of fun, a waitress recalled. Rusnak was a 'sipper', not a drinker, and a bit of a 'dufus – hunky but not too smart.'

At home Rusnak was a family man who did voluntary work, mowed his lawn and owned a Labrador called Barney. When his children, Alex and Katie, came along and began to attend the local Shrine of the Sacred Heart School, he was invited on to the school board, an advisory body that met once every two months. Linda walked the children to school and brought baked food to monthly parent-teacher meetings.

David Cronin lived just a mile away on the other side of Interstate 83, the highway that suburban commuters used to get into the city centre. The two families attended the same Catholic church, the Shrine of the Sacred Heart. The intimate grey-stone church served a small Baltimore parish of just 750 families. Cronin's children went to the same school, and the bank treasurer was also a member of the school board. Rusnak was also a member of the local golf club, where he played off an 18 handicap, and he and Cronin sometimes enjoyed a round of golf together. All in all it was quite a neighbourly relationship for a currency trader and his boss.

Rusnak continued to make bad bets on the foreign exchange markets. At the beginning of 1999 he took a bold step to cope with his growing losses. He persuaded Bob Ray and David Cronin to let him do his trading through other banks. This allowed Rusnak to enter into agreements with various banks to act as his prime brokers in the international currency markets. The banks would accumulate all the spot foreign exchange trades into one forward foreign exchange trade between the prime broker and Rusnak, and settle for cash in dollars at a fixed date every month.

It was an extraordinarily daring notion. Prime brokerage accounts were more commonly used by hedge funds, not by lone traders in regional banks. Regional banks in America did not normally allow traders to gamble their money through such accounts. The Baltimore bank was a subsidiary of a national bank in another country, but it behaved as a US state bank in every other way. It did not have the infrastructure for serious foreign currency dealing through prime brokerage accounts. Even AIB's treasury business in Dublin did not use prime brokerage accounts.

Cronin and Ray went along with the idea, however, agreeing with Rusnak that it was time to expand the scope and scale of his trading and to ease the burden on the treasury's back office. The two senior executives helped him set up the accounts. Sales people from New York banks came to Baltimore to check him out and look at the bank's credit record. Prime brokerage accounts can only be set up with the bank's authority, which Rusnak's bosses provided. This arrangement allowed Rusnak to outsource some of the back office functions, such as the regular valuation of the outstanding options on the bank's books and the reporting of these deals. It gave him the scope to execute large volumes of high-value currency trades with the financial houses he selected, Bank of America and Merrill Lynch, which he later changed to Citibank when his Merrill Lynch sales contact moved there.

It also gave him greater opportunities to hide his activities. Rusnak entered fictitious prime brokerage transactions into the books and records of the bank and then 'amended, cancelled or reversed those transactions before the monthly net settlement with a prime broker, thereby allowing him to conceal his actual trading losses and to maintain his ability to continue trading on behalf of the bank', according to the US Attorney for Maryland, when later charging Rusnak with fraud.

Working through these banks, Rusnak used a foreign exchange product known as a 'historical rate rollover' to covertly roll losses forward. In a typical rollover the dealer would apply the historical rate of a maturing contract to the spot end of a new pair of contracts, thus extending the maturing contract and deferring any gains or losses. This tactic was used in 1986-87 by an Australian trader, Andy Koval, who was considered a foreign exchange genius until it was discovered that he had lost his company AU$50 million.

In 1995, the Foreign Exchange Committee, a group of specialists that advised the US Federal Reserve in New York on foreign exchange market issues, warned in its annual report, available on the Internet, against banks allowing traders to use historical rate rollovers as they entailed 'considerable financial risk.'

On top of this unusual arrangement, Rusnak started to occasionally ask the back office to perform what he called 'controlled settlements', an irregular practice of withholding payments of trades so as to eliminate any risk to the bank in relation to the settlement of a contract.

In the spring of 1999 there was a chorus of protest about the new arrangements from within the treasury. Jan Palmer, senior vice-president in charge of treasury operations administration, complained about the controlled settlements to David Cronin. Lawrence Smith, who was responsible for verifying Rusnak's trades, complained about his inability to obtain confirmations for transactions for the prime brokerage accounts. Treasury risk control complained that the feature of the prime brokerage accounts that allowed Rusnak to net trades each day made it impossible to ascertain if there had been off-market trades with a particular counter-party during the day.

Cronin called a crisis meeting. It was attended by Bob Ray, Rusnak, his trading supervisor, the head of risk control, and the head of the back office. It was by all accounts a tempestuous encounter. Rusnak, backed up by Ray, protested that the back and middle office staff did not understand how the prime brokerage accounts worked. He put on a display of temper, berating the back office and, according to contemporaneous bank documents, threatening to have back office employees fired. Following the meeting Cronin directed Ray to bar Rusnak from using the prime brokerage accounts for a while.

Victims of Rusnak's bullying during this tense time sent e-mails to the head of the back office. These were brought to Cronin's attention. The treasurer called another meeting, this time to ask that treasury staff 'treat each other more respectfully', according to Ludwig, who said that it appeared 'that the treasurer took no significant action.'

After a month, when the net transactions had been confirmed, Rusnak was allowed to resume trading as before. This time, however, Cronin insisted that in future there should be a daily audit trail of each trade in the prime brokerage accounts, and Ray agreed that he and Rusnak's supervisor would review all of Rusnak's trades 'and the rationale behind each trade'. The back office meanwhile established in writing that it was not responsible for confirming individual prime brokerage account trades, but would confirm the net daily settlement. But no daily audit trail was carried out, there was no evidence of a scrutiny of each trade made by Rusnak, and the back office did not always confirm the net daily settlement. In addition, throughout the whole year the internal audit, headed by Michael Husich, did not take a single sample of Rusnak's transactions to check if it had been independently confirmed.

A couple of months later trouble bubbled up again for Rusnak. In mid-1999 managers took him to task for going over his risk exposure (Value at Risk) limit of $1.5 million. This was the largest loss the bank could anticipate suffering as a result of Rusnak's trading activities under adverse market conditions. Calculating Value at Risk is the main method used by banks to monitor their foreign traders' activities. AIB's Baltimore subsidiary relied upon a model developed by AIB to measure the likely losses it would incur through foreign exchange trading. The model used 'Monte Carlo' simulation techniques to generate 1,000 hypothetical rate fluctuations and calculated the resultant profit or loss in foreign exchange forward dealings. The Value at Risk is the tenth-worst outcome. The system was considered to be 99 per cent accurate. It was the only statistical basis for briefing documents supplied to the key bank committee charged with monitoring risk, the Asset and Liability Committee, of which Cronin was chairman. AIB had set a policy that Allfirst's foreign exchange trading limit should be no higher than a relatively conservative $2.5 million, of which Rusnak was allocated $1.5 million (later increased to $1.75million). This was the largest loss the bank could reasonably anticipate suffering if the markets moved against its trading position. The system showed that Rusnak was exceeding his risk limit by up to $1 million every three months or so, though in reality he was constantly breaching the limits by far more than this.

The Value at Risk method was, in any event, rendered useless as an alarm system because Rusnak entered false information into the bank records in the form of bogus options that appeared to hedge his real positions. Throughout the whole time Rusnak worked for the bank the model consistently failed to detect a problem. He also entered foreign exchange forward transactions in Devon, the system used to record prime brokerage account trades, but reversed them before the monthly settlement date.

When the managers queried Rusnak about the few times he exceeded the risk limit, he complained that the system he used to check his own risk was too cumbersome. In response the bank's computerised system to measure trading risk was partly redesigned by the risk-control department to make it faster and easier, and a copy of the application was installed in Rusnak's computer in an effort to 'hopefully avoid future over-limit situations', according to an internal bank memo addressed to Rusnak and later leaked to the *Wall Street Journal*. The memo added that it was Rusnak's responsibility to know his Value at Risk at the end of each day.

Rusnak used another device to manipulate the Value at Risk calculations. Notwithstanding his bogus options, he often had huge open currency positions. The bigger these were, the higher the Value at Risk would be and he would be seen to be exceeding his limit. The system recorded these as 'hold-over' transactions, deals that traders enter into towards the end of the day as the markets are closing but which are held-over for settlement until the following day. He gave a spreadsheet containing the false figures from his personal computer to the employee who was supposed to independently check the Value at Risk every day. The fake figures supplied by Rusnak were never, however, entered into the bank's software. Despite the frequency of his hold-over transactions, no one ever checked to see if the transactions figured in the next day's trading activity at the rate at which they had been recorded.

In one three-month period, AIB finance officials would later establish, hold-over positions were used on fifty-two occasions out of fifty-eight trading days that were sampled. 'The fraud was so inelegant that on some occasions Rusnak would leave the same hold-over position running for three straight days. No one caught it,' said Ludwig.

When the trading manager, Rusnak's immediate supervisor, left in 1999, the treasury funds manager, Bob Ray, decided not to hire a replacement. Costs were being squeezed throughout the bank. Rusnak was told to report directly to Ray in future – the trader's protector and patron had now become his direct supervisor.

Cronin depended on Ray to monitor Rusnak's trading activities but while Ray was a highly regarded bond trader, he did not have the same knowledge of foreign currency trading. Nor did he increase his focus on Rusnak's proprietary trading after the manager left. This further diminished the control capabilities of what was now a clearly dysfunctional treasury in a bank often in turmoil over staff changes.

Staffing levels to monitor controls were already minimal. Internal auditing devoted at most two full-time auditors to audit the entire treasury department. The risk assessment department amounted to only two people who were responsible for assessing risk at the bank. Treasury risk control assigned just one full-time employee to measure trading risk in the foreign exchange portfolio. As time went on this latter post was given to Svetlana Tslav, 25, who had not long before completed her master's degree in finance at Johns Hopkins University in Baltimore. She had a finance degree from the School of Professional Studies in Business and Education of Johns Hopkins and was certified by the Global Association of Risk Professionals as a financial risk manager. Rusnak once told her not to worry about the bank's limits which he was regularly exceeding.

'They walked around the hallways for about a year, and Lana would say, "Hey, John, you are over your limits today." And John would say, "Don't worry, Lana, I will take care of you",' a source within the bank told the *Baltimore Sun*.

For a few months late in 1999 Rusnak apparently won some money back through his new prime brokerage arrangements, and was thus able to reduce his bogus option positions with some big bets. But it didn't last and the losses began to rise again, only this time the curve was steeper as the stakes were greater and he was taking bigger positions to try to win back his losses. Despite the brief winning streak, by the end of 1999 he had gambled away another $48.2 million of the bank's money, taking his total losses over three years to almost $90 million. But he was again showing a net trading profit on the balance sheet, this time for an estimated $1.049 million, and he took home another six-figure bonus of $122,441 at the end of the year, on top of his salary of $104,000.

10
Johnny Ruz,
Making a Move

The next year several events occurred, any one of which could have exposed Rusnak, but astonishingly the trader survived them all.

The first involved something that he could not have foreseen. One of the American banks with which he had just opened a prime brokerage account got worried about the size of his transactions, and raised its concerns directly with AIB in Dublin.

Due to the extraordinary way Allfirst had successfully resisted attempts by AIB throughout the 1990s to monitor the internal activities of its wholly-owned American subsidiary, the treasury operation in Allfirst was not audited by AIB, unlike all the other foreign operations of Ireland's biggest bank. AIB group treasurer, Pat Ryan, had to rely on information from David Cronin about what was going on in Allfirst. The limits Ryan set were so modest that it was difficult to conceive that an Allfirst trader might have already gambled away $90 million of its money.

In March 2000, however, an official at Citibank contacted Ryan about a large gross monthly prime account settlement that was due to be made with Allfirst. Citibank was one of the banks with which Rusnak had entered an arrangement to act as a prime broker in the international currency markets. Citibank accumulated all the spot foreign exchange trades Rusnak made in one month into one forward foreign exchange trade that was to be settled on a fixed date each month for cash. The date was coming due and Citibank was concerned about the size of the settlement which, the official told Ryan, amounted to more than $1 billion. Could Allfirst cover the transactions?

Ryan assured Citibank it could, but, according to Ludwig, he asked Allfirst's risk assessment staff to make a 'discreet inquiry' about the matter. On this occasion he did not call David Cronin, the head of Allfirst treasury and his one-time colleague, with whom he regularly discussed inter-bank matters. A member of the risk assessment staff reported back to Dublin that the Allfirst treasury had recently entered into a prime account with Citibank, that the transaction was to be a net settlement (i.e. it was in reality much smaller), and that the $1 billion was more than offset by a larger figure owed by Citibank. The staff member also told Brian King, executive vice-president of the Allfirst risk assessment group, about the Citibank inquiry.

King later said that he took the matter to the top in the bank. He provided notes he had prepared showing what Ludwig referred to as 'apparent conversations' with Frank Bramble in which he alerted the Allfirst chairman to the Citibank inquiry and the explanation of the $1 billion settlement, as well as the apparently negative attitude of Bob Ray, Rusnak's boss, to inquiries about his traders. Bramble told the Ludwig inquiry that he did not recall such conversations with King, and produced his calendar to show he was on vacation on one of the dates mentioned in King's notes. He said, however, that he did remember conversations from time to time about Ray's behaviour and that on one occasion he told David Cronin that it would have to change or he would be fired.

King's detailed notes were highly critical of the treasury operation and the environment there, Ludwig said, noting drily that 'we are not certain' if King's notes were used in the meetings. A former colleague of King recalled that he was not just a meticulous notekeeper but 'a real head-office staffer', and that 'it was inconceivable that he would not have shoved information like that up the line, to cover his ass.'

Evidently both Pat Ryan in AIB and those who knew at Allfirst were satisfied with the explanation of the $1 billion settlement and no one made an issue out of Rusnak making such large monthly trades.

Around this time a new opportunity was given to Rusnak to evade controls. The trader persuaded treasury to install a Travel Bloomberg system on his laptop to allow him to trade at home and on holidays. This was contrary to the rules applied in any foreign exchange trading operations. Currency traders are required by US law to take a holiday off-site and off-line for ten consecutive trading days once every year, so that someone else can work in their place and during which time irregularities could come to light. Trading from home is generally forbidden but these rules never applied to Rusnak.

'It's hard to understand why they ever allowed that,' said a banker familiar with Allfirst. 'Only the head of a very large operation would be allowed to go on-line from home, and then only if he needed to know what was happening around the world, not a minor guy like Rusnak. Why would he need to be in global contact?'

There was another event in the same month that could also have alerted Dublin to something amiss at its American bank. This was the annual filing of accounts by Allfirst with the Securities and Exchange Commission in the United States, known as 10K filings. The accounts filed on 16 March 2000, and indeed the accounts for the previous year, clearly showed that the notional value of Allfirst's foreign exchange trading was in the billions of dollars.

Rusnak was by this time becoming careless about the output from his 'fake docs' file. Sometimes he would print off confirmations that did not match the trade he had supposedly executed. In June 2000 a back-office staffer asked why there was no confirmation for a trade Rusnak had recorded at an earlier date. Rusnak produced a confirmation showing that the trade was executed on the day the staffer had questioned it, not the day it was booked. But the staffer in the back office accepted the late confirmation without drawing the obvious conclusion, that it was entered into the system only after a query had been raised. A sense of lethargy about monitoring trades apparently prevailed in the back office after long experience of management taking Rusnak's side in any dispute.

The following month, however, a risk assessment staffer raised a concern about the fact that daily currency rates were not being independently verified by the back office. Rusnak had taken care to ensure that they would not be independently verified. He had insisted that the currency rates should be downloaded from the Reuters terminal to his PC's hard drive before being fed into a database available to the front and back office. He argued that he needed access to the rates to monitor his Value at Risk, and he had at one time suggested creating a feed into the database from his computer.

Incredibly, his proposal had been adopted. The treasury risk control analyst explained this to the risk assessment analyst who in her notes of their meeting wrote: 'This is a failed procedure' and 'technically the trader/s could manipulate the rates.' She also asked why the treasury operations could not obtain the rates separately. The control analyst told her that the bank would not pay $10,000 for a data feed from Reuters to the back office, due to the bank's cost-cutting drive. There the matter rested for a time.

Though the practice of not confirming off-setting pairs of Asian options was by now well established, Larry Smith, who was responsible for confirming his trades, claimed that in the first half of 2000, a meeting of senior treasury staff members formally decided not to confirm all of Rusnak's trades, though it remained the bank's official policy to confirm all trades. The reasons were the difficulty of doing so in the middle of the night, and fact that no net cash payment was involved. Ludwig noted, 'We have been unable to confirm this account with any of the other alleged attendees.'

In August 2000 Rusnak came very close to exposure again. Out of the blue an internal audit of treasury operations decided to check trade confirmations in treasury, a practice that had long been neglected. They sampled 25 transactions to see if they had been confirmed properly. Most were low risk trades. They only sampled one foreign exchange option. It was one of 63 foreign exchange options on the books at the time of the audit. The option selected for sampling turned out to be genuine. Later it would be learned that roughly half of the rest were bogus. If they had checked one more of Rusnak's options the probability of discovery would have increased to 75 per cent, Ludwig calculated, two more and the odds would have increased to about 86 per cent and four more would have taken the odds to 95 per cent. But, unlike his currency bets, the odds against being caught out by bank staff seemed to be stacked in Rusnak's favour.

Similarly when the treasury risk control and credit risk review offices were made aware that Rusnak had breached by $86 million the $100 million foreign exchange credit line that AIB and Allfirst had set for his dealings with a particular bank, it was simply put down to 'trader error' and no one questioned why Rusnak had incurred an exposure to the bank (UBS) as large as $186 million. Similar instances of 'trader error' piled up but no one bothered to query them because by the time they were discovered the trades had been settled and the overages eliminated. Nor did anyone ever try to reconcile Rusnak's daily profit and loss with the general ledger. If they had, they would have found that it swung wildly and frequently exceeded his stop-loss limit of $200,000 a month.

Near the end of that year, another opportunity to improve the technology in the treasury was missed, apparently, as before, because of budget constraints.

David Aaron, a sales representative who worked for a technology company called DerivaTech, heard on the brokers' market – the traders' grapevine – that Rusnak was looking for a better risk management system. Aaron's company sold a state-of-the-art system called DTRisk that could assess the various risks to a trader's port-folio from things like interest rate moves in the market or a decline in the value of the dollar. A trader could, for example, instantly find out what the impact on his position would be if the dollar were to decline 2 per cent in the coming week.

Aaron travelled from his New York office to Baltimore to discuss the project with the currency trader. He found Allfirst to be 'a small regional bank, with a very close-knit group of congenial traders, not aggressive like New York banks, a place where a trader who had finished his finer days could easily go and work for quite a while.' He and Rusnak went for lunch to Peter's Pour House. 'Rusnak was quite a nice guy,' he recalled. 'He had time for me when I went down there. He took me out to lunch and we spent an hour or two talking busi-ness. He said he had a need of better tools to risk-manage. We went through the typical type of sales talk.' Aaron would not say later how much the system would have cost Allfirst, but indicated it would be around $500,000. Some time later Rusnak spoke to Aaron on the telephone. The bank would not be buying the system because of budget constraints, he said.

By now Rusnak was the talk of trading rooms around the world. In Asian banks he was becoming a recognised player. Even when he made his trades through Citibank and Bank of America, dealers in the Far East would recognise his play and say: 'Hey, that's Johnny Ruz, making a move.'

But throughout the year his losses were mounting faster than ever and he was not able to show much of a profit, despite the ever-growing bogus options. For the year 2000 his net trading profit was only an estimated $800,000 and his annual bonus fell to $78,000. In the previous twelve months he had gambled away another $211 million of AIB's money, more than $4 million a week. A total of $300 million had now slipped through his fingers and, as yet, no one at Allfirst or AIB had noticed that anything was wrong.

11

Peter's Pour House

By the start of 2001, Rusnak reckoned that of the three hundred people globally engaged in high-level foreign exchange trading, one hundred were proprietary dealers, and of these he was among the top ten. He was consumed by how important he was.

The big banks were by now seeking him out for special treatment. In June 2000 Rusnak was entertained at the US Open golf championship at Pebble Beach, California, where Tiger Woods won by fifteen strokes. He was accompanied at Pebble Beach by Mike Bernal, then head of corporate foreign exchange sales at Bank of America's San Francisco office. Rusnak was taken to Las Vegas for a spell of gambling and he and his wife, Linda, were flown to Italy for a holiday. When FBI agents examined his passport later they discovered that he had travelled extensively in four continents.

In January 2001, sales representatives from Lehman Brothers took him to the Super Bowl, the annual American football extravaganza held that year at Raymond James Stadium in Tampa, Florida. Tickets were at a premium everywhere but especially in Baltimore as the Baltimore Ravens were playing the New York Giants. Rusnak was among the 72,000 spectators cheering the Maryland team on as Baltimore trounced the Giants 37-7.

Two months later, on 14 March 2001, he found himself being fêted at the annual Robin Hood ball in the Jacob Javits Centre on Manhattan's West Side. The dinner was organised by the Robin Hood Foundation, a New York charitable foundation started in 1988 by three rich young Wall Street traders. It was the once-a-year occasion for traders from all over America to dress up in tuxedos and let their hair down together. That evening, Hollywood actress Gwyneth Paltrow introduced the Red Hot Chili Peppers from the stage as the traders mingled with moguls like Rupert Murdoch. Rusnak's reputation was by now so well established as a big player that fellow currency traders and salespeople sought him out. People lined up to talk to him. They wanted him to deal with them. He was so important that his recommendations could help traders and sales representatives get good jobs.

Big traders bring in profitable business and banks expect their foreign exchange salesmen to do everything to pamper them to keep them trading. The foreign exchange business in the United States is unregulated and there are no securities regulations to prevent banks spending lavishly on traders who bring in good profits. Rusnak was considered a hot property by the banks with which he did business and for which he was making big money, especially Bank of America and Citibank. A $1 billion settlement would be little more than a computing exercise for Citibank yet it brought in $10,000 in commission and imposed other charges on forward transaction rolls. A $1 billion trade was nothing to Rusnak now.

Even from afar, the banks looked after Rusnak. Sometimes he would arrive at Peter's Pour House with a bunch of traders. At the same time the telephone in the bar would ring. The caller would say, 'That trading group, take care of them.' Everything they ate and drank would then be charged up to one of two credit card numbers kept on scraps of paper by the cash register. One was an American Express card number ending in 21004 in the name of 'Anthony Piccolo'. This was a pseudonym for a salesman from one of the big banks, according to a source close to Rusnak. The other was for a Visa card ending in 8145 in the name of 'Richard Marra'. Rusnak at the time dealt with a Citibank sales representative of that name. Marra worked for Merrill Lynch until 2000 when he switched to Citibank. Rusnak moved his business from Merrill Lynch to Citibank at the same time. At the more expensive restaurants he was taken to there were $100 bottles of wine and the bills would come to thousands of dollars.

The threat of discovery loomed again in January 2001. Allfirst's independent auditors demanded confirmation of an option contract that Rusnak had entered in the books. It was a yen-dollar options contract with a strike price, or agreed-upon exchange rate, of 84 to 1, and an expiration date of 8 January 2001. After some delay, Rusnak told them that the confirmation could be obtained from a person called David Russell. He worked in Suite 162, 2472 Broadway, New York, for a counterparty by the name of RBCDS FX.

The bank sent a letter to the New York address asking David Russell to confirm the options contract. A reply came back in early February, signed by David Russell, vice-president of the RBCDS FX, confirming the contract.

However, there was no David Russell and nor was there any counterparty known as RBCDS FX.

On 20 January Rusnak had rented a mailbox at 'Mail Boxes', a small walk-in postal shop situated between an optometrist's and a hair stylist's at the upper east end of Broadway in Manhattan. According to the Mail Boxes files, he made the application by telephone, giving his own name and Baltimore address and credit card number, but listing David Russell as a second person authorised to receive and send mail. 'Suite 162' was simply box number 162 of 400 square brass letter boxes along the wall of the shop. When the independent auditors wrote to David Russell the letter was forwarded to Rusnak at his home address. He replied to it, signing Russell's name, and then had the reply posted from New York. It was the only letter that passed through Suite 162, as far as staff could remember. The confirmation was accepted as genuine.

Rusnak was soon faced with a new problem. His use of cash from the Allfirst balance sheet was growing along with his losses, and from January 2001, at Cronin's direction, it was charged to trading income and included in treasury and Allfirst management reports. The management report showed that foreign exchange trading revenue appeared to have more than doubled from $6.6 million to $13.6 million, but that net trading income had only increased by about $1.1 million, demonstrating that Rusnak was seemingly using more of the balance sheet but getting little in return. Following inquiries from audit and internal finance about this, Bob Ray instructed Rusnak to reduce its usage, according to Ludwig. Rusnak now needed to find a way of getting his hands on a new source of funds.

When Nick Leeson came under pressure to raise big money his solution was to start selling so-called straddles, or options based on movements in the Nikkei index of Japanese stocks. By selling large numbers of these options on very attractive terms, Leeson was able to generate significant amounts of cash in the form of premiums. He continued to sell these options even though he lost heavily on them because they were a way for him to obtain cash quickly and defer risk.

Rusnak's solution was to sell so-called deep-in-the-money options to some of the world's biggest financial institutions. Rusnak would get large cash payments, running to tens of millions of dollars, from the counterparties, by selling similarly large liabilities in the form of yen-dollar options that would come due at a later date. The options had exercise prices far above the value of the currency involved. These payments were also known in the business as 'synthetic loans'. He negotiated a European variation of this form of option, i.e. it would be exercised at a fixed date – a year and a day in the future – rather than at any time. This would buy him some time to put the money to use to try to retrieve his losses. There was one drawback. When he sold the 'deep-in-the-money' options, the counterparties would set exchange rates for their repayment in yen that were almost certain to make them huge profits. Put simply, the deals gave Rusnak a huge up-front premium in exchange for high interest rates.

For the first 'deep-in-the-money' options contract he turned to Citibank where his friend Richard Marra worked. A year beforehand, Citibank had agreed to act as one of Rusnak's prime brokers, and had sought and received an assurance from Pat Ryan, the group treasurer of Allfirst's parent bank AIB, that Allfirst was able to meet a settlement of more than $1 billion. Secure in the knowledge that Ireland's biggest national bank was prepared to underwrite Rusnak's mammoth trades, Citibank struck a deal on 20 February 2001 to give Rusnak $125 million cash at a strike rate of 73.77 yen to the dollar, in return for an option that would expire in one year and one day. That is, Citibank purchased the right to buy US dollars from Rusnak at a future date at 73.77 yen to the dollar. The yen at that time stood at 116 to the dollar. If the dollar did not fall quite dramatically before the option expired, then Rusnak would have to repay much more than $125 million. He was agreeing to sell dollars 35 per cent cheaper than they were dealing for cash settlement and thus he needed a 35 per cent decline in the dollar for the option to expire worthless and for him to get to keep the entire $125 million – so unlikely as to effectively make the option a high-interest loan.

There was, in fact, an outside chance that Rusnak might pull it off. The American economy was heading for recession, the Nasdaq bubble had burst and US Federal Reserve chairman, Alan Greenspan, had begun a rate-cutting spree. According to the text books the dollar should have started to decline on the world markets, but it was stubbornly refusing to do so and this would continue until mid-2002.

The option Rusnak sold was now a huge liability of Allfirst and it was recorded on the books as a liability. Rusnak had to get it off the books quickly. He did that by recording a bogus deal with Citibank that gave the impression that the original option had been re-purchased. He would repeat this process with four other banks before the year was out, each time saddling the bank with massive unrecorded liabilities, so that he could get cash to finance his increasingly desperate efforts to win back his losses.

In the same month that he was securing his synthetic loan from Citibank, Rusnak's trading activity again came to the attention of AIB in Dublin. The AIB group's financial reporting unit, when preparing the year-end 2000 financial reports, raised questions about the extent to which Rusnak was using the bank's assets, and about the size of the cash flows generated by his activity. Allfirst's controller and the bank's director of financial reporting also had questions to ask of Bob Ray, head of treasury funds management and Rusnak's direct boss. Staff members of Michael Husich's audit team also wanted to know from Ray what was going on. Ray evidently explained the purported strategy behind Rusnak's trading activity, and said it was 'relatively low risk'. This information was passed on to AIB group financial reporting but nothing more was done. As had happened before, Ray had again saved his trader from exposure.

Shortly afterwards, Rusnak started negotiating a second synthetic loan, with Bank of America. He wanted $75 million, partly to pay off a huge debt of $50 million he owed Bank of America. But this one did not go so smoothly, and was nearly his undoing.

When Bank of America quoted an exchange rate for the option, Rusnak protested that it was too high, and that the loan deal would cost Allfirst $600,000 more than it should. He sent a blustering e-mail to his contact in Bank of America threatening to close his prime brokerage account: 'I have come to you with a problem, we need to outsource our balance sheet funding,' he wrote, according to a leaked account of the e-mail in the *New York Times*. 'You have the numbers. It is easy enough for you to figure out the P&L [profit and loss] consequences if we pull the entire relationship. This is the deal-breaker. I am playing golf tomorrow at noon. If I don't have a revised proposal by then, I will close the prime brokerage facility and cease speaking to any of your desks.'

The reply was equally blunt. It came from Michael Bernal, the head of corporate foreign exchange sales in Bank of America's San Francisco office. 'You are $50 million behind,' he told Rusnak, according to the *Financial Times*, 'You are going to do the deal.'

Bernal asked a superior, Hugh 'Beau' Cummins, head of global foreign exchange at Bank of America, to call AIB which, the *Financial Times* report said, was understood to have told David Cronin in Baltimore to move ahead with the deal. AIB denied that this happened in the way that the newspaper described. Nevertheless the deal went through.

A year later, after the fraud was uncovered, a Bank of America executive who was authorised to speak about the trade, told the *Irish Times* that Bank of America officials, including their client manager who dealt with AIB, raised the deep-in-the-money option with 'senior AIB executives' in Dublin early in 2001, after which the deal was approved. 'They actually went to Dublin,' the executive said. 'The trade was an unusual one. It was a deep-in-the-money trade, the only one done with Bank of America of this nature. Discussions arose about how the deal should be priced and Allfirst – and I guess Rusnak – was unhappy with that pricing. He became really belligerent and threatened to take business away, and for Bank of America that kind of response was quite confusing and confounding. The e-mail [he sent] was made available to Allied Irish [Banks] executives. Senior executives at Allfirst and Allied Irish [Banks] came back and said to Rusnak the price quoted by Bank of America is fair, the deal will go through. I think he had his wrists slapped.' The Bank of America executive added, 'This is incredibly sensitive. Allfirst and AIB remain a client. The reality is that discussion took place.'

Following publication of this account of events in the *Irish Times*, senior sources close to AIB protested that there was no record in the bank of the trade being raised at parent-bank level. 'People are convinced this just didn't happen' the sources said, adding that the transaction was 'never an issue'.

Contacted again, the Bank of America executive repeated that the meeting with AIB did, without question, take place in Dublin. She rang back some time later to say it might have been a conference call.

Ten days later the *New York Times*, again quoting a Bank of America executive, also reported that Bank of America consulted AIB about the trade, after which an Allied Irish Banks executive approved the deal. The report went on to say that this meant 'Allied Irish [Banks] was aware that Mr Rusnak was seeking these loans outside the bank to finance his trading and that knowledge probably should have raised questions in the parent bank about what Rusnak was doing.' It also noted that AIB denied that such a conversation took place with Bank of America.

In his report Ludwig said that he found no oral or documentary evidence at Allfirst and AIB to substantiate the *Irish Times* account and 'a representative of Bank of America has advised Allfirst that the press account is false.' The former Comptroller of the Currency later told the *New York Times*, 'I know AIB looked at this very seriously and has not been able to find any internal record of the contact.'

However, in his internal investigation in Allfirst and AIB, Ludwig came across evidence of an e-mail in which Rusnak informed one counterparty that, 'I have come to you with a problem, we need to outsource our balance sheet funding,' the same wording used in the e-mail Rusnak sent to Bank of America that the bank said was passed on to AIB. The categorical statements of Bank of America that the issue was raised with the parent bank, and the denial by AIB of any record of the contact, points to the possibility that the issue was again handled 'discreetly' within AIB.

A source close to Rusnak gave the trader's version of events. The source said Bank of America 'put the screws' on Rusnak for a really bad deal. His attitude was, 'I'm not this desperate to let you screw me, go to hell!' Once Bank of America 'smelled the deal' however, they wanted it so badly that they contacted someone in the AIB treasury in Dublin, threatening to pull their business from AIB because of the trader in Baltimore. AIB then contacted David Cronin who told Rusnak, 'I don't care how bad the deal is, just do it.' The deal went through on 7 March 2001 at hugely advantageous rates for Bank of America, with Rusnak getting a $75 million premium at a strike rate of 75 yen to the dollar.

Rusnak felt that the traders sensed his vulnerability. They smelled his fear. They believed that he was in so deep he couldn't win, and they felt they could shove deals down his throat. 'They are the guys that really ripped off Allfirst,' a friend said bitterly.

That same month Brian King, the executive vice-president responsible for risk management, may have tried to alert Allfirst chairman, Frank Bramble, about the dangerous situation in treasury. King kept detailed notes of his conversations. His contemporaneous notes, according to Ludwig, 'suggest' that in March he discussed with Bramble 'or at least intended to discuss with him', the importance of separating those charged with profitable trading from the control functions. Once again Bramble told Ludwig he did not recall such a discussion.

Within weeks of the Bank of America deal, Rusnak again came close to exposure. The previous year a staffer working for King had discovered that the source of daily foreign exchange rates supplied to the back office was not independent, meaning a trader could manipulate the rates, and those employed to verify his transactions would have no way of knowing. Rusnak had insisted that the currency rates should be downloaded to his PC's hard drive from the Reuters terminal, before being fed into a database available to the front and back office.

In April, at the end of the first quarter of 2001, the staff member asked Rusnak to e-mail her the spreadsheet to check the rates. She immediately discovered the system was corrupt. The cells for the yen and the euro still had links to Rusnak's computer. Accordingly, in the first quarter Risk Assessment report, Control Market Risk was downgraded from 'good' to 'weak'. This downgrade lowered the overall 'Quality of Risk Management' rating to 'acceptable'. The problem was brought to the attention of Cronin, King and Ray. The 'chosen solution', as Ludwig put it, was to create a computer disk to download prices from Reuters directly to the back office, using Rusnak's computer terminal. But nothing was done, despite prodding from King's staff. The downgrade was repeated at the end of the second quarter. Only in October, a year after the bank discovered that the source of daily currency rates was not independent, was the problem fixed.

AIB trading experts would subsequently discover that Rusnak had in fact been manipulating the currency rates up to April 2001, to make it look as though he was trading within the monthly stop-loss limit of $200,000 set by Ray, but no one had attempted to find out if he had been doing so. This figure was the maximum loss Rusnak could run up in a single month. Once this point was reached, Ray and Cronin would be informed and Rusnak would have been prevented from doing any further trading for the rest of the month.

The stop-loss figure was now totally irrelevant. In early May 2001 Rusnak executed four transactions – two with Citibank and two with Bank of America – that involved a total of about $1.6 billion in notional value. This sum was so large that it was noted on trading screens around the world. It moved markets, Rusnak told a friend.

Not long after the $1.6 billion trades, the extent of Rusnak's trading was brought to the personal attention of AIB's chief executive officer, Michael Buckley, in Dublin. A 'market source' who did not refer to specific trades or to Rusnak by name, suggested to AIB in late May that Allfirst was engaging in very heavy foreign exchange trading, said Ludwig. The market source was not identified in the Ludwig report. A bank insider said that the market source had alerted a senior executive in AIB who in turn had brought it to Buckley's attention. The AIB group chief executive telephoned David Cronin in Baltimore to ask about the matter.

After getting Buckley's call, Cronin went directly to Rusnak. The Allfirst treasurer wanted to know from him what was going on, as 'Buckley was all over him', the trader later told a friend. Cronin, he recalled, told him that Buckley had been informed in Dublin that Allfirst was getting really aggressive in the foreign exchange markets and that the biggest foreign exchange trader in North America was working out of Allfirst.

Rusnak told the Allfirst treasurer about the large trades. Cronin got agitated. He said that he had to report the figures back to Buckley. He prepared a memo and, according to Rusnak's friend, had his secretary e-mail it to Rusnak to check the figures before sending it to Dublin. Rusnak recalled that the figures in the memo were net rather than gross and even then were too low.

Cronin called Buckley back and told him that there had been no unusual or extra large transactions in the previous two weeks. He sent his reply in the form of a memo to Buckley on 25 May: 'To bring closure to our conversation earlier today about foreign exchange turnover, I confirm that we have had no unusual or extra large transactions in the last two weeks with counterparties locally or with

London. Our daily average turnover in this period was $159 million. To the extent that someone who spoke to you has anxieties with respect to our activities, it could be explained by our concentration of turnover with two institutions, i.e. Citi[bank] and Bank of America. We transact 90 per cent of our dealings via 'prime' clearing accounts with these banks. This is done to minimise counterparty exposure using a monthly netting arrangement. It is ironic that initiatives to minimise one risk can understandably be misinterpreted as giving rise to another.' Cronin's memo was 'a forceful and categorical denial of any problem,' said Ludwig, and 'this response satisfied AIB.' Ludwig discovered that in the weeks following the memo, the turnover figure was at least three or four times greater than the $159 million.

The concern raised by the market source to AIB was not passed on to Allfirst chief executive, Susan Keating. Buckley told Ludwig that it was his practice directly to call an executive in charge of a matter.

In mid-June, Cronin asked Rusnak for daily reports on the number and notional amounts of proprietary foreign exchange transactions. These reports, supplied to Ludwig, confirmed that Rusnak was an extraordinarily active trader, who traded instruments with notional positions totalling hundreds of millions of dollars, and sometimes billions, each day – on some days reaching nearly $4 billion. 'This was nearly twenty times the amount the treasurer told Mr Buckley was the daily turnover in response to his May 2001 inquiry,' noted Ludwig. The daily volumes were so high that Cronin's 25 May reassurance to Buckley that 'satisfied AIB' was almost immediately made redundant and misleading.

There is no evidence that daily figures were sent to Dublin. Rusnak recalled to his friend that Cronin said he had to send daily reports to AIB after Buckley's inquiry, and that the task of sending them was assigned to an official called Fred Boos. Rusnak does not know if they were sent. When asked later by the *Irish Times* if AIB requested daily accounts of the volumes of trades at Allfirst from around mid-summer, the answer from AIB's law officer, Bryan Sheridan, was 'no'. Rusnak told his friend that the senior officials who knew about the crisis over the Buckley telephone call were David Cronin and Bob Ray.

Much later, after he had been found out, Rusnak commented to his friend regarding the whole episode, that if he was still trading after that, well, one could draw one's own conclusions.

Rusnak expressed the view that his bosses may not have known exactly what he was doing or how he was doing it or what the numbers were, but that they didn't want to rock the boat because if the real numbers came out the desk would get closed, any losses would be disclosed and they would get into trouble as they knew he was trading well over the internal limits. Everyone in the markets knew what he was doing. Traders were a tightly-knit group. They didn't know if he was winning or losing, but they could probably figure out that he was getting desperate when he was betting $1.5 billion in a night.

Cronin gave Rusnak promotion in June 2001. Despite his poor earnings record the previous year, and notwithstanding the tantrums and the crises which were now regular occurrences, and ignoring the fact that he was regularly exceeding his limits, Rusnak was given manager-director rank and put above the trader responsible for doing straight-forward foreign exchange for bank customers.

The mounting losses played more than ever on Rusnak's nerves and for the last year he was in a state of constant panic. The strain also began to tell at home. He would sit up late trading with Asian markets on his laptop with its Travel Bloomberg system. He couldn't sleep, he was drinking and it was causing strains on his marriage.

Matters had got steadily worse for him as the year progressed. In early autumn the SEC, the powerful body which regulates companies and markets in the United States, inquired about the unusual cash flow related to foreign exchange activity. The Allfirst financial reporting unit determined that Rusnak had large offsetting foreign positions. It asked internal audit to pay special attention to trading in an upcoming treasury audit due in three months.

Time was running out. But he still had some lives left.

The end almost came one day in early December when the supervisor of Larry Smith, the back office employee responsible for verifying Rusnak's trades, dropped into Smith's office and noticed two trade tickets lying on Smith's desk that did not have confirmations attached. When asked for the confirmations, Smith said the trades did not require confirmations as they cancelled each other out and were with Asian counterparties. The supervisor reminded Smith that all trades should be confirmed and pointed out that the trades did not offset each other as they had different expiry dates. The supervisor subsequently told Ludwig that he directed Smith to confirm the two Asian option trades and all trades in future. Smith for his part claimed to the bank investigator that the supervisor told him simply to look into the possibility of confirming the two trades.

Around the same time, David Cronin ordered that the currency trading balance sheet be reduced to below $150 million.

Rusnak continued to make bad bets as 2001 drew to a close. Yet despite the alarms and excitements throughout the year drawing attention to major problems with his trading he was still able to raise another $100 million cash in synthetic loans in December to meet his ever-escalating losses. He got a premium of $25 million from Deutsche Bank on 6 December, another $25 million from Merrill Lynch on 12 December, and $50 million from Bank of New York on 24 December.

By the end of the year his total losses had soared to $674 million. But on the books he was showing his biggest ever profit for the bank: an estimated $1.3 million. This entitled him to his biggest bonus ever, $220,000, on top of his salary which was now $112,000 for the year. The bonus was due to be paid on 8 February 2002.

12

Panic at the Bank

With the New Year, events began to close in on Rusnak, but not before yet another chance was missed to catch him out.

In January 2002 a member of the financial reporting team at Allfirst sent year-end reports to AIB for inclusion in a AIB group submission to the Central Bank of Ireland. It showed open foreign exchange positions with a value greater than $100 million. Again AIB contacted David Cronin about his problem trader. The Allfirst treasurer asked another finance officer to look into it. After talking to Rusnak the officer said the prime brokerage account positions were incorrectly reported, as they had been valued at their trade date whereas he should have used year-end values.

When David Cronin returned to the bank in January after a Christmas holiday in Ireland, he checked the currency trading balance sheet and saw that it had been reduced to below $150 million as he had directed. But in the middle of January it suddenly spiked upwards in one day to over $200 million. At that time he found that the December turnover in foreign exchange trading was a whopping $25 billion.

Evidently in some agitation, Cronin told Bob Ray that Rusnak's trading positions might have to be closed down. He asked the head of treasury funds management to ascertain what it would cost to do that. Ray calculated that it would cost $500,000 to do it immediately, or $300,000 to close them down gradually over a few weeks. Cronin and Ray subsequently gave conflicting testimony to Ludwig about what was decided. Cronin said he told Ray to close down Rusnak in two weeks. Ray said that Cronin expressed the intention to halt Rusnak's trading on 1 February for an indefinite period and to allow his positions to come off the books over time thereafter.

The matter came to a head at a staff meeting on 28 January. Cronin announced that Rusnak's position was being closed down.

Ray was uncharacteristically quiet and at the end of the meeting, by Cronin's account, he asked: 'That's it then? We're continuing to close down Mr Rusnak's positions?' When Cronin confirmed his instruction, Ray said he expected that Rusnak would quit his job.

This was a very serious step. Usually a trading desk is closed down only if it has gone 'under water' and has to be closed down before it gets worse. Surprisingly, Cronin did not inform Keating, to whom he directly reported.

Two days later, on Wednesday 30 January, after the back office supervisor heard Rusnak's positions were being closed, he checked with Larry Smith and discovered that Rusnak was still trading a small number of options. When Smith showed him two deal tickets the supervisor again noticed that no confirmations were attached. Smith admitted they had not been confirmed as they offset each other and involved Asian counterparties. The supervisor reminded Smith of his instruction in December to confirm all trades, including the Asian option deals. He ordered the clerk to review all the option tickets. There were twelve in all, none of which had been confirmed. The supervisor ordered Smith to stay in the South Charles Street headquarters office that night to confirm the options with the Asian counterparties.

As darkness fell in Baltimore the Asian markets began to open. Smith started making the telephone calls. One by one the banks and finance houses in Asia entered as counterparties informed him that they did not have the currency options on their books or, equally alarming, that they did not trade such options at all.

Incredibly, when Rusnak came to work the next morning, Thursday 31 January, he was summoned to the back office supervisor's room and simply told that Larry Smith was 'having trouble' confirming the trades. Even at this stage, faced with evidence of his fraud, Rusnak successfully stalled for time. He said he would call the broker who had handled the trades and obtain confirmations by the next morning. He did not give the broker's name or telephone number to enable Smith to do the confirmations independently. Working late and alone, Rusnak called up his 'fake docs' file and entered names and figures on the screen, then printed out twelve documents, complete with logos, purporting to be confirmations from the Asian banks.

When Smith came to work on Friday morning, 1 February, he found that Rusnak had left the twelve written confirmations on his desk in the back office, matching the twelve options trades. The back office supervisor arrived and examined the confirmations. He thought they looked suspicious. He called a meeting with Rusnak and Bob Ray, and told Ray that the options would still have to be confirmed by telephone.

It was a tempestuous meeting. Ray, ever protective of Rusnak and his trading, retorted that the failure to get confirmations was a back office problem and that it was their job to track them down. For his part, Rusnak put on yet another show of anger. He was making money for the bank. If they continued to question everything he did, he would quit, he said, and stormed out of the room. After he left, the supervisor showed Ray the confirmations that Rusnak had left on Smith's desk. Ray agreed the confirmations looked odd, but warned that Rusnak might leave because of the scrutiny, and that jobs would be lost in the back office.

Ten minutes later Rusnak returned to the office and promised to help confirm the trades. But as the Asian markets were now closed for the weekend, they would have to wait until Sunday afternoon before he could provide them with the telephone number of the broker who had arranged the trades. Then he left the bank to go home.

With verbal denials from the twelve counterparties in Asia and grave suspicions that the documents were fake, it was now impossible not to conclude that the bank had a rogue trader on its hands.

It would be another three days, however, before the top executives of the bank would be officially told. 'The temptation is not to go up the line until you have the facts,' said a bank insider offering an explanation. 'Their lives were passing in front of these guys. They were trying frantically to get some way around it.'

Rusnak, too, was frantically trying to find some way around it, but he reckoned that 'the end-game was over.' He heard that a team of auditors from AIB had arrived at the bank in late January, possibly 28 January, and were going through treasury documentation. They refused to talk to him. This was the day Cronin started to close him down. He began to think everything was connected. He reckoned they had panicked in Dublin after an AIB trader in New York had lost up to $10 million and had been fired, and they were now checking out all their trading desks, including Allfirst which had not had an AIB treasury audit since 1994. A woman trader had indeed been fired in New York two months beforehand. She had been trading in so-called stripped mortgages. Her losses were still being 'washed out' at the time, but they were in the $6 million to $10 million range.

On Sunday Rusnak did not keep his promise to telephone the office with the number of the broker who could confirm the trades. There was, of course, no such broker. When Larry Smith called at midday Rusnak told the back office employee that he would not have the broker's number until nine o'clock in the evening. Smith and two senior colleagues kept calling his number until the early hours of Monday morning but Rusnak did not come to the telephone. Cronin and Ray made one last desperate attempt to get their trader to sort things out by driving to his house in Mount Washington. Rusnak was not there.

Keating and Bramble were told on Monday afternoon.

It was soon clear that the twelve outstanding options were not the whole problem. As the treasury began closing down Rusnak's desk, a call to the Bank of America to settle a trade was met with confusion, according to a later report in the *Wall Street Journal*. Bank of America had no record of that options trade. The executive faxed the confirmation slip for the trade to the Bank of America for inspection. The trade had been documented out of Bank of America's Singapore office. The office there did not generally confirm option trades, and the telephone number listed on the receipt turned out to be that of a Singapore law office.

After AIB group treasurer Pat Ryan and his team arrived in Baltimore on Tuesday evening it was established that there were nineteen bogus transactions with Asian counterparties on the books and five real option transactions with counterparties that had been removed from the system with bogus liquidating positions.

In the first three years when things started to go wrong, Rusnak's losses had been comparatively modest. At the start of 2000, when Citibank first alerted AIB to the extraordinary level of foreign exchange trading at Allfirst by asking if it could cover a $1 billion settlement entered into by Rusnak, the losses still amounted to less than $100 million. That year Rusnak had lost $300.8 million. In 2001 he more than doubled that to $674 million.

The final figure of $691,204,113 consisted of $291.6 million in bogus assets and $397.3 million in unrecognised liabilities, along with $2.3 million in legitimate trading losses incurred by Rusnak in January 2002.

Through it all Rusnak had shown a yearly profit on the balance sheet. His bonus cheque for 2001 of $220,456 was due the following Friday 8 February. Now it would be torn up by the bank.

13
Brogue Trader

John Rusnak knew he had two very important things to do as he made his way home with the cardboard box of his possessions that Friday evening, 1 February. He had to break the news to his wife and he had to get a good lawyer.

The first was the most difficult. Linda was a very religious person. Both were church-goers. John had been brought up a Catholic and they attended Sunday mass at the Holy Shrine of the Sacred Heart Catholic Church. He had to confess to Linda what he had kept from her for five years, that he had been accumulating and hiding losses and counterfeiting trades at the bank. He now faced prison for losing the bank a staggering sum of money and for accepting his salary and bonus during those years. There would be no bonus, and no more salary. He was out of the bank.

That Sunday he had been invited by the salesman of a New York financial house to another Super Bowl extravaganza in Florida, to watch New England play St Louis. He did not go. There would be no more junkets now. The salesmen would be distancing themselves from him as fast as they could.

Instead he drove Linda and their children, Katie and Alex, to a Maryland hotel not far from Baltimore where there was a pool in which the children could amuse themselves as he told her what had been going on. Her response was to tell him that if he didn't get straight, she would leave him. He promised he would and that there was no question of fleeing to escape the consequences, and they returned home to Mount Washington on Monday.

The next task was to find a lawyer. Rusnak was in very serious trouble, facing anything up to thirty years in jail when the full extent of his fraud was uncovered. He sought out Bruce Lambdin, in Cockeysville, an outlying suburb of Baltimore not far from where he lived. He knew of Lambdin because he worked in the same building as Mitch Lambro, a civil attorney and the husband of a good friend of Linda's. Well known on Baltimore's golfing circuit, Lambdin was in fact the wrong type of lawyer for the emergency situation Rusnak faced. A specialist in drug and drunken-driving cases who described his work as 'your basic sex, drugs and rock 'n' roll', he had little experience in cases that would involve federal law enforcement agencies. But he knew other lawyers who had. He advised Rusnak that this was a job for a close friend, a lawyer with the unlikely name of David Beckham Irwin.

David Irwin, a six-foot-four former top-flight athlete with a passion for softball, had a reputation as Baltimore's best criminal lawyer. The 54-year-old attorney was a partner in the firm of Irwin, Green, Dexter and Murtha, which had its offices in a small detached house within walking distance of the courthouse in Towson, in Baltimore County north of Baltimore city. Despite its modest trappings, the firm had handled some of the highest-profile criminal cases in the city in recent years. Irwin's defence of a lorry driver who killed his wife after finding her in bed with another man resulted in the defendant getting only an 18-month work-release sentence. The gangling, bespectacled lawyer came to national attention when he and a partner, Joseph Murtha, successfully defended Linda Tripp, the federal employee in Washington whose secret recording of the confessions of a White House intern, Monica Lewinsky, in 1997 helped build a case for impeachment against President Bill Clinton. Tripp was charged with violating Maryland's laws on wire-tapping but the case was dropped when the two lawyers argued that Lewinsky, the state's main witness, was just out to get their client. Most important from Rusnak's point of view was the fact that Irwin had worked as a prosecutor for the US attorney's office in Baltimore from 1980 to 1985 and he knew how the federal authorities operated. He adopted a low-key approach, not alienating people as he went along, to get the best results.

Lambdin called Irwin on Tuesday and they set up a meeting for Thursday with the trader who had almost wiped out the second-biggest bank in Baltimore. However, events overtook them. After bank officials established on Tuesday that many of Rusnak's trades were bogus, Allfirst's lawyer called the Federal Bureau of Investigation to inform them of the suspected fraud at the bank and

the absence of a trader. Two FBI agents, Kevin Comiskey and Steven
Graybill drove out to Rusnak's house on Tuesday evening. They
established that he was there and was not fleeing with the bank's
money. When the story broke the next morning with Michael
Buckley's announcement on Irish radio – well before dawn in
Baltimore – the lawyers' meeting with Rusnak was hastily rescheduled
to late Wednesday morning in Irwin's office in Towson. Irwin invited
Comiskey and Graybill to sit in. As they talked in a ground floor
reception room, with the FBI agents taking notes, Frank Bramble
and Susan Keating were telling journalists at Allfirst headquarters in
downtown Baltimore that they did not know where Rusnak was and
that the FBI was looking for him.

Rusnak later told a friend that he spoke by telephone with security at the bank around 5.00 pm on Tuesday, the day before the press
conference, and told him he had hired a lawyer. Irwin and Lambdin
also set out to squash any perception that their client was a fugitive
or had stolen any of the missing millions. They told journalists that
Rusnak had, in fact, been at home with his family or with friends
when he was described as missing. 'He's not a fugitive, he's here in
town and he isn't going anywhere,' Irwin told reporters.

That afternoon, Irwin and Lambdin brought Rusnak to the US
attorney's office in Baltimore for a meeting that went on for some six
hours with two US attorneys, Steve Schenning and Steve Dunn.
The two FBI men again sat in. Rusnak seemed eager to confess right
away to everything. A friend of Rusnak's also attended the meeting,
and was unhappy that Irwin seemed to be moving too fast in the
direction of conciliation. But Irwin calculated that stonewalling at
this stage would be counter-productive and that the decision Rusnak
was now making would affect his future life. He got Rusnak to turn
in his passport to show that he was acting in good faith and would
maintain contact. He had talked to Mitch Lambro who assured him
that Rusnak was unlikely to run away.

There was a helpful leak from an agent of the FBI in Baltimore in
the *Wall Street Journal* on Friday 8 February. The paper said that
Rusnak had met FBI agents and explained to them that he had made
a series of bad investments on behalf of the bank and had then tried
to develop a strategy to recover the losses before the bank officials
discovered them. The FBI did not believe Rusnak embezzled the

money but that he had tried to recoup losses in the markets and just got in deeper. 'He hung around Baltimore,' the FBI official told the *Journal*. 'It isn't looking like he embezzled $750 million and has an island in the Caribbean.'

FBI agent Peter Gulotta told the *Irish Times*, 'It's not as though the guy is walking out of the bank with a gun in his hand. White collar crime is different from violent crime where you want to make sure you get him off the street.'

Irwin realised from what Rusnak told him that the Allfirst version of the story was not so simple, that there was another side to it, that the controls at Allfirst were not up to scratch and that perhaps there was collusion of some sort by other bank officials trying to cover their failures. His insistence that his client had neither stolen any of the missing money nor ever been on the run went a long way to creating an image of Rusnak as a victim of his own foolishness and lack of controls at the bank rather than as a fraudster. Meanwhile AIB was emphasising that Allfirst was the victim of a 'devious, complex and determined' fraud. In Dublin, AIB group chief executive Michael Buckley told a reporter, 'His lawyer has been very clever putting it in people's minds that if you have not got the money in your bank account then it isn't fraud. Well I don't know about that.' Irwin also told journalists that he believed that the sum lost would not be as large as the bank had said. The next day Allfirst stated that the total losses were $691.2 million, rather than $750 million.

The trader turned over everything he had relating to his bank activities to the FBI. This included his laptop hard drive. It contained details of his trading from home and while travelling in the eighteen months since the bank equipped his portable computer with the Travel Bloomberg system. The Allfirst chief executive was apparently unaware that Rusnak often traded late at night at home: Susan Keating had told reporters at the press conference in Allfirst headquarters on 6 February that he was not permitted to trade at home. The hard drive, Rusnak believed, also contained a draft of the message David Cronin had sent Michael Buckley the previous May in response to the AIB chief executive's query about a high level of foreign exchange trading at Allfirst.

For Rusnak at least the days of panic and sleepless nights worrying if he would be caught were at an end. He was glad it was over and

felt an incredible relief. He was thinking now only of his wife and
children. He had got to deal with the guilt. He felt awful about his
friends being drawn in to the scandal. Nevertheless he hoped that
what emerged would show other people's involvement. Unlike
Nick Leeson, who wrote a bestseller about the Barings Bank scandal
called *Rogue Trader*, he was not going to write a book. He did not
want to profit from it and he didn't want to drag his family through
it all again.

Rusnak had to face a dire financial future. He was pretty frugal
when he was earning good money and had some savings and the help
of a supportive family. He was relieved that he hadn't been arrested
and that the FBI did not regard him as a fugitive in any way. He
handed over details of his bank accounts to agents so they could
establish that his spending was well within his salary and bonuses.
They quickly accepted that he was not an embezzler with bank
money hidden away. He was allowed to stay unsupervised at his own
home, despite the enormity of the losses. A key sign that they trusted
him was that the investigators didn't seize his assets. He knew from
Irwin that if he told the FBI something untrue they were going 'to
kill' him. He realised his colleagues would be hurt but he was doing
what was best for himself. John and Linda Rusnak's neighbours and
family rallied around protectively. Many dropped by the house to
commiserate. 'It was like a wake,' said one, 'with people even bringing food.'

For several days the Rusnaks had to cope with a media stake-out
which made the family virtual prisoners. Shortly after the news broke
early on Wednesday morning the first reporters showed up at the end
of the short drive leading to his house on Smith Avenue.

Another John Rusnak, a retired steel-worker who lived in
Edgemere, Baltimore, spent much of the first day telling reporters
who telephoned that they had got the wrong man. One Irish woman
'asked in a heavily-accented brogue whether I had embezzled
$750 million,' he said, greatly amused.

It was a major international story, even making the pages of the
Russian newspaper, *Pravda*, which editorialised: 'There are too many
ambiguities in this story: Why, for example, did the leadership
contact the FBI only after Rusnak did not come to the office? It
probably did not want to wash its dirty linen in public.'

Reporters called at neighbouring houses asking residents for their views on Rusnak. Margery Pozefsky, of the non-profit Baltimore Clayworks ceramics and cultural centre, said he was on her board. 'He seemed like a nice guy, but he was always distracted by work. At least I assumed it was work. He kept volunteering to solicit contributions from people in the banking industry, but he never really came through. I always got the feeling that he didn't really have the connections to people that high up.'

So many photographers positioned themselves at the Shrine of the Sacred Heart School to try to get pictures of the Rusnak children or of the currency trader coming to collect them that the school was closed for a day and parents told to keep their children at home. The day after that parents and teachers blocked the parking lot entrance with their cars.

One of the worst moments for Rusnak came on Ash Wednesday. The photographers were still there with their long-range lenses, hoping to get a picture of a penitent Rusnak with ash on his forehead. Rusnak refused to oblige them. He had another reason for not been pictured going to church. Every jerk who did something wrong picked up a bible, he told a friend, and it would look as if he was using religion to depict himself in a better light.

Rusnak resigned from the board of the Shrine of the Sacred Heart School, and also gave up his membership of the golf club: he could no longer afford it. Parishioners who encountered him at the church were 'very non-judgmental', said the pastor, Father Richard E Cramblitt. 'People weren't casting aspersions. I noticed a lot of people saying supportive words. It was something quite beautiful. They were concerned for someone who was clearly in trouble. It's hard to understand how could anyone lose that amount of money and create such a furore. Everyone was saying how clever and sophisticated he was, and I don't doubt that, but at the same time he's not an evil man. He got in trouble and got scared and did dumb things to cover up his mistakes, just hoping the currency market would turn around and make a profit and pay it back.'

Rusnak was also counselled by the 'Preaching Pastor' the Rev Joe Ehrmann, a tall, white-bearded minister at Grace Fellowship, a non-denominational evangelical church in Timonium, just north of the Baltimore beltway, with a mission 'to glorify God and to spread the

news of Jesus Christ to Baltimore and the world.' The Rusnaks sometimes went there instead of the Catholic Church (Linda's father had
been a Methodist minister). Ehrmann, a former star defensive line-
man with the Baltimore Colts in the National Football League, ran
a foundation for disadvantaged youth called Building Men for Others
and was an icon in the African-American community. He got
Rusnak to help set up an urban football league for disadvantaged kids
for the autumn 2002 season, by using the trader's business skills to
acquire equipment and get charitable donations.

With Rusnak not talking to the media, reporters outside his
house were reduced to jotting down details of a typical domestic
scene in suburban America: an American flag drooping from the
balcony, children's toys lying around, two wooden sledges, two pogo
sticks, an oval hand-made ceramic tile at the end of the driveway
bearing the family name and address. Several reports referred to
Rusnak as 'Mr Middle America'.

It took an analyst at Gimme Credit in New York to make the
obvious bad pun. Its report on the affair was headed 'Brogue Trader'.
The name never stuck. Rusnak was not Irish. He had never even
been to Ireland.

AIB group chief executive Michael Buckley. (*The Irish Times*)

David Cronin, 'fooled' by Rusnak. (*The Irish Times*)

John Rusnak on the balcony of his Baltimore house after the discovery of fraud.
(*The Irish Times*)

Facing the media: AIB chief executive, Michael Buckley and AIB head of corporate communications, Catherine Burke, leaving the press conference at the bank's Dublin headquarters on 6 February 2002, the day it announced the fraud. (*The Irish Times*)

AIB deputy chairman John McGuckian (*The Irish Times*)

Susan Keating, posing for an Allfirst promotional photograph. (*The Irish Times*)

Lochlann Quinn, AIB chairman, makes a point after the report on fraud by Eugene A Ludwig (right), 14 March 2002. (*The Irish Times*)

Bank investigator Eugene A Ludwig and colleague Duncan Hennes leave the press conference after presenting their report, 14 March 2002. (*The Irish Times*)

The Velvet Hammer: Susan Keating explains how John Rusnak defrauded the bank, at a press conference in Baltimore on 6 February 2002. Beside her are Allfirst chairman Frank Bramble (left) and AIB's group treasurer Pat Ryan who was sent to Baltimore to assess the damage. (*The Irish Times*)

Shareholder protest: AIB shareholder, Niall Murphy, takes the platform at the bank's annual general meeting in Belfast in May 2002 to protest about the fraud. He is later removed by the two security men standing at the back. Michael Buckley (left) and Lochlann Quinn (right). (*The Irish Times*)

John Rusnak after being charged with bank fraud on 5 June 2002. (*The Irish Times*)

14

Not the Barings Bank

On Tuesday afternoon, 5 February, the day before the losses at Allfirst were announced, shares in AIB closed at €13.62. Things were going well. The bank's stock was popular with Irish and international investors. On the Irish stock market the AIB group was valued at €12 billion, making it the biggest Irish company in terms of market capitalisation. It had enjoyed that status for just a few days. Élan, the Irish pharmaceutical giant, had been the Republic's biggest company until the *Wall Street Journal* published a critical account of its accountancy practices. In the climate of intolerance towards companies thought to be manipulating numbers after the collapse of the Texas energy-trading company Enron, investors had unloaded Élan stock, driving its value down by more than 50 per cent.

Throughout Tuesday, Buckley still did not know how bad the news would be. He could only wait for the figures from Baltimore.

AIB had been through this before. In 1984 the then AIB chairman, Niall Crowley, had to brief the Taoiseach, Garret FitzGerald, about another calamity for the bank, the pending collapse of the Insurance Corporation of Ireland. Then, too, AIB needed the government to provide assurances about the ability of the bank to weather the storm. Similarly, Crowley did not know the full extent of the damage at the time, other than that the bank was facing losses of between IR£60 million and IR£130 million and could be brought down. On that occasion the bank had been rescued from collapse when the State bought ICI for a nominal sum and AIB wrote off its IR£85 million investment. It was an astonishing action for the government to take and still rankled with the Irish public.

ICI was founded in 1935 to undertake general insurance business. By 1981 it employed 800 people and was preparing to announce its eighth successive rise in profits to IR£8.5 million. AIB was so impressed that when the US insurance company, Continental Corporation, put its 7.99 per cent of stock up for sale, the bank seized the chance to buy it. Despite the poor economic climate in Ireland, the bank was doing well and looking for opportunities to invest – this was just before they began the acquisition of First Maryland in Baltimore. ICI was the second-biggest non-life insurer in Ireland and an acquisition would allow AIB to move into the insurance sector and expand into Britain where ICI had 70 per cent of its business. AIB steadily increased its stockholding. By October 1983 ICI was under its control and ownership. But the feeling of triumph in AIB's boardroom dissipated when profits for 1983 were revised downwards from IR£7.9 million to just IR£2 million.

Because it was involved in a contested bid for the insurer, AIB had never been given access to the company's books, relying instead on figures and projections provided by ICI's accountancy firm Ernst & Whinney. It did not undertake due diligence, the most basic prerequisite for an acquisition. The bank now discovered to its utter dismay that ICI was grossly underfunded. AIB had to transfer IR£5.6 million to cover claims from policy-holders, a sum that rose to IR£18 million as the extent of the liabilities became clear.

The problems were mainly at ICI's rapidly-expanding London branch. Rumours circulated that ICI was taking on the type of business other insurers would not touch because of the high risk. It was said to have insured American bloodstock and amusement parks, and even telegraph poles in Australia that were destroyed in a bush fire. In the first year of AIB ownership, it wrote down IR£200 million worth of insurance business, some twenty times more than in the previous twelve months, leaving ICI open to an enormous increase in potential claims.

By October 1984 AIB was facing a potential disaster. It dug deep to transfer another IR£40 million to avert ICI's collapse. A team of bank investigators found that the situation was so bad that AIB would have to write off its entire IR£86 million investment and liquidate ICI. At that time the total amount of funds AIB held on behalf of its shareholders was IR£227 million. ICI's losses could run into hundreds of millions and AIB itself was facing ruination. The situation was so grave that Niall Crowley was forced to call for help from the government, and inform the Central Bank of Ireland and the Stock Exchange of the looming catastrophe and the implications for the Irish economy.

This was the second financial debacle threatening the State's financial fabric that Garret FitzGerald's Fine Gael-Labour coalition government had had deal with. Two years earlier it had stepped in to sort out a horrendous mess created by the failure of the PMPA insurance group. The Central Bank advised FitzGerald that the scale of ICI's losses was so great that the entire banking system was in danger of collapse and that there could be a run on the Irish currency.

AIB's board of directors had decided that the best way to protect the bank's shareholders was to cut its losses and put ICI into liquidation. But this would wipe out insurance cover for 120,000 policies in the Republic, 30,000 of which were for motor vehicles. It insured one-in-four Irish companies for accidents and liability claims. It provided insurance coverage for big state-owned companies including the national airline, Aer Lingus, and the national transport service, CIE. If the insurer were to be liquidated the country could literally grind to a halt.

Crowley went to the government to bail it out. At the time FitzGerald was sick at home in Palmerston Road, Dublin. AIB claimed that the only remedy was for the State to acquire ICI and take over its liabilities, then estimated at between IR£50 million and IR£120 million. FitzGerald reluctantly led a rescue mission. Many critics believe he panicked and ultimately let AIB emerge too lightly from a calamity of its own making.

In March 1985 ICI was acquired for the State at a nominal sum and placed under the control of the Minister for Industry, Trade, Commerce and Tourism. AIB wrote off its IR£85 million investment. The government set up a special fund forcing all Irish banks, including AIB, to provide 15-year loans to cover the losses at a low interest rate. The rival banks were enraged at having to save AIB from a problem of its own making. AIB was not asked to pick up the full cost of the debacle.

The AIB chief executive, Gerry Scanlan, admitted that their acquisition turned out to be a 'lemon' though it had looked at first like a 'jewel'. (The phrase 'jewel in the crown' was often used by AIB executives to describe Allfirst.) AIB shareholders were appeased with the payment of a dividend – another act considered outrageous by taxpayers who were picking up the ICI bills, though FitzGerald protested in his autobiography that none of the ultimate cost was borne by the taxpayer.

AIB described its actions as 'responsible', leading Tomás MacGiolla, leader of the Workers' Party, to comment in the Dáil that when people were being 'responsible', it meant that 'they are standing by the big boys.'

Niall Crowley later claimed that AIB had 'successfully' disengaged from ICI, confirming the widespread view that the terms of disengagement had been excessively favourable to the bank. The same strategy of paying dividends to shareholders to signal that it was business as usual and that the bank was undamaged was followed after the Rusnak losses. In 2002, however, the bank was in a stronger financial position and could withstand huge losses in its American subsidiary. The biggest danger was that a serious fall in its share price as a result of the scandal would make it vulnerable to a takeover by another bank.

AIB group treasurer, Pat Ryan, whom Buckley had sent to Baltimore to work out how much the bank had lost, rang the AIB chief executive a number of times on Tuesday 5 February as the work progressed. At one point he indicated that the losses could be of the magnitude of about $300 million. But the audit team kept finding new unmatched trades. Buckley told Ryan he needed a figure that he could stand over. The bank could not afford to announce one figure and have to revise it upwards in a few days time. They needed as much certainty as possible if they were to establish their credibility in the markets in the days after the news was announced. Very late that night Ryan came through and said it looked like the final figure would be $750 million.

Michael Buckley, his closest colleague, Gary Kennedy, AIB's head of finance, Catherine Burke, head of corporate communications, and public relations consultant, Jim Milton, prepared a statement for the Dublin and London stock exchanges to restrain the level of panic and contain the damage. During the night and early morning Burke and Milton rehearsed answers that might be anticipated from the media and analysts. They had to reassure the markets that AIB could withstand the setback, and try to confine the extent to which the price of its shares would fall. Above all, they had to play down any similarities between what had happened at Allfirst and at Barings Bank. The investing public still had a vivid memory of how Barings customers and shareholders suffered when the bank collapsed in 1995 after Nick Leeson's fraud was uncovered. AIB did not also want a run on the bank.

Shortly after 7.00 am a statement headed 'AIB investigates suspected fraud at Allfirst treasury operations' was issued to the stock markets. It announced the losses and suspensions and said that experienced senior AIB treasury personnel were in Baltimore and had taken over day-to-day responsibility for Allfirst treasury. The consequences of these losses for AIB Group's 2001 earnings were a once-off reduction of €596 million after tax, it said. The events would not have any impact on the dividend policy and capacity of AIB Group. AIB's tier-one capital ratio would be reduced from 7.2 per cent to 6.4 per cent and Allfirst's from 10.5 per cent to 7.2 per cent. These remained strong by international financial standards. It was a case study in damage limitation. On RTÉ radio Buckley got a chance to address the Barings Bank comparison before the markets opened when Cathal MacCoille asked him, 'From what we know this far does this look like another Nick Leeson affair?' Buckley replied, 'Well I think there is one very important respect in which it is not a Nick Leeson affair. What Nick Leeson did caused terminal damage to Barings. I think it is very important that I make the point here this morning for our customers, our staff and our shareholders, that even when we write off that $750 million we will be making a profit after tax for 2001 of €400 million. I said this is a heavy blow to the bank but this is by no means a fatal blow and business will continue as usual as far as customers are concerned and as far as our staff are concerned.'

The markets were unconvinced. AIB shares plunged in value in Dublin and London as soon as the trading day began. During the day they fell by more than 20 per cent as nervous investors dumped the stock amid speculation that even if the bank did not collapse, its share value was going to be lower. The shares recovered some ground by close of business with the scale of the loss reduced to 17 per cent.

Analysts expressed themselves mystified by how the whole thing could have happened. Experts who could decipher the complex technical explanation of how the fraud was perpetrated by using bogus foreign currency options found it difficult to understand the enormity of the losses.

At 11.00 am, with the bank's monitors showing that AIB shares had lost €1.52, falling to a price of €12.10, Buckley faced reporters from all over the world at the bank's Ballsbridge headquarters.

Jim Milton, who usually preferred to remain in the background, guided journalists to their seats and negotiated space with camera crews. A week earlier he had hastily convened a press conference for another client, the DCC corporation whose chief executive, Jim Flavin, had been accused of inappropriately dealing in shares at the fruit distribution company Fyffes just before the company issued a surprise warning that its profits were about to slump.

Looking exhausted, Buckley and Kennedy fielded a barrage of questions. They suggested that Rusnak might not have acted alone and perhaps was aided by an accomplice either at Allfirst or in another financial institution. 'There are some indications, but only some, that there may have been some collusion with this individual with either somebody else within the organisation or some external parties,' said Buckley. 'But our first responsibility is to identify the cash amount that we are out, to make a determination of what that is, to deal with it and to let the markets know, and let the markets know that while this has been a blow, that AIB is still very strongly capitalised and that the basis on which we are doing business has not been undermined.'

Buckley stressed that the bank was itself still seeking answers at this early stage. He emphasised that the fraud would not affect the solvency of AIB. He was 'very comfortable' that $750 million was the total extent of the fraud and that mechanisms had been put in place to limit the losses. But by 12.30 pm the shares had fallen to €11.46 with no sign of any let-up in selling.

In the afternoon the Taoiseach reinforced Buckley's reassurances. Customers had nothing to worry about, he said. Their deposits were safe. 'AIB will still be profitable. The bank's 98,000 Irish account holders would not suffer any loss of funds. There's no danger to any AIB account holders of any loss of funds.' A government spokesman said state intervention was not being considered.

When the markets finally closed at 5.30 pm AIB shares had fallen €2.27 to finish at €11.36. Within one day's trading AIB had followed Élan on a downward trajectory and by the close of trading had been overtaken by its closest rival, Bank of Ireland, as the largest Irish company on the Dublin Stock Exchange. Some €2 billion was wiped off the stock market value of AIB, reducing its capitalisation from €12 billion to €10 billion. Bank of Ireland was worth €11.2 billion. To lose to Bank of Ireland was particularly hard to take.

Buckley assembled a group of lieutenants to support and advise him in the immediate aftermath of the Allfirst fraud. They included Gary Kennedy, Colm Doherty, the head of the AIB capital markets division, and Eugene Sheehy, head of the retail bank's operations in Ireland. Alan Kelly, the head of investor relations, was also associated with the management of the evolving crisis. They kept deliberations so confidential that many other senior AIB executives learned about day-to-day developments from the media and the Internet. The nine-member group executive committee, selected and headed by Buckley, which runs AIB, was responsible for setting policy and implementing strategy across the bank. It reported to the chairman and board of directors and ultimately bore responsibility for what had happened anywhere in the group, including Allfirst. As well as Buckley, Kennedy and Sheehy, the committee included Frank Bramble, the head of the bank's US operations. In January Susan Keating had joined this elite group for the first time. Buckley was the first chief executive in the history of AIB to promote a woman to such a high position. Irish banks had long been criticised for their failure to promote and nurture female managers despite the disproportionately large number of women employees.

Just eight months after taking the top job at AIB which was to be the high point of his career, Buckley was fighting to survive. People who know the 57-year-old Cork man said his genial exterior masked a steely interior. Colleagues described him as very disciplined with a high work rate and grasp of detail. 'I have a lot of energy; I'm blessed for my age. It hasn't been getting me down,' he said shortly after the fraud was announced.

Buckley was an unlikely banker. He studied for the priesthood for two years at the Catholic seminary in Maynooth, Co Kildare but later switched to the National University of Ireland as a student of philosophy. 'It took me about two years to discover women – and what they might do to you,' he once said in a radio interview. 'There was a fundamental crevice between being a priest and having any sort of relationship with women.' He was now married and he and his wife, Anne, had two daughters and a son.

His career in finance began when he worked for the Department of Finance where he helped write national budgets. In the evenings he studied for a master's degree and taught political philosophy at University College Dublin. He moved to Luxembourg in 1977 as *chef de cabinet* for Michael Murphy, president of the European Court of Auditors. After his return to Ireland in 1981 he was recruited from the state sector by multi-millionaire financier Dermot Desmond to work for his stockbroking company, NCB Stockbrokers, where he quickly rose to managing director. A former colleague there said he was 'the most unflappable guy he had ever seen in that job.' Buckley was involved with Desmond in promoting Dublin's derelict docklands as an international financial services centre. NCB won lucrative contracts to handle the flotation of semi-state companies and when the company was sold to Ulster Bank, Buckley became a millionaire.

In 1991, Tom Mulcahy, then head of AIB's capital markets division, recruited Buckley to the bank and three years later Buckley took over from Mulcahy as CEO of AIB capital markets. He successfully argued Ireland's case in Europe against Germany to preserve a double taxation agreement that proved crucial for the development of the international financial services centre.

In 1999, Buckley was appointed head of AIB's banking operations in Poland. AIB had secured a foothold in post-communist Poland by acquiring Wielkopolski Bank Kredytowy and that year Buckley supervised its merger with Bank Zachodni, leaving AIB in control of the fifth-biggest bank in Poland. The bank had exposure to very substantial bad debts, which raised concerns for investors, some of whom blamed Buckley for creating new risks. Poland gave Buckley the retail experience a future chief executive would need. He took up residence in Warsaw and kept up a punishing schedule, commuting to Dublin at weekends and travelling to attend board meetings at Allfirst and Singapore-based Keppel Tat Lee Bank. 'That has been very tough on a personal level for me and for Anne,' he said. 'Most of our staff have young families, which is much tougher.'

When he was appointed AIB chief executive on 1 May 2001, colleagues hoped that he would herald a new era for the bank. He had not been associated with the DIRT tax evasion or the ICI crisis.

Now the AIB chief executive was himself the subject of much criticism in the Irish and international newspapers. There was speculation that heads would roll at the very highest level. 'The Buck-ley has to stop somewhere,' said a *Daily Telegraph* headline. Takeover rumours began circulating.

Then the unexpected happened. The share price began to rise again two days after the news broke and by 20 March it had fully recovered. It was a remarkable comeback. Some large investors paid tribute to the bank's deft handling of the crisis. But the single biggest factor that dragged the share price back up was the persistent rumour that a bid might emerge for AIB, possibly from Royal Bank of Scotland. Senior AIB executives insist it never received an approach from Royal Bank of Scotland or any other bank about a takeover in the days after the losses were announced. Shares in AIB had risen sharply three years earlier on rumours of a takeover by Frankfurt-based Deutsche Bank. Other banks such as the Dutch banks, ABN Amro and ING, and Lloyds TSB were also mentioned. Deutsche Bank was said to be prepared to pay around €19 billion for AIB. Nothing came of it all and the London Stock Exchange launched an inconclusive inquiry into the source of the speculation, which had given some speculators a windfall. AIB chairman, Lochlann Quinn, dismissed the rumours as 'the stuff of newspapers.' One banker suggested that they were fuelled by someone close to AIB precisely to lift the stock price, though such a tactic could evolve into a self-fulfilling prophecy.

But a chink had appeared in AIB's armour. Royal Bank of Scotland, Barclays or Lloyds TSB could be tempted to take advantage. Royal Bank of Scotland also had interests in the US where it owned Citizens Bank, the biggest bank in New England, and was anxious to make more acquisitions. Allfirst, with its businesses in the mid-Atlantic states, might fit its portfolio. The rumours were definitely not emanating from its boardroom, Royal Bank of Scotland chief executive, Fred Goodwin, told the *Irish Times*. They owned Ulster Bank and did not feel the need to do anything more in Ireland. But he refused to comment on whether Allfirst was on its shopping list.

In March, just a month after the AIB fraud was uncovered, the new chief executive of the rival Bank of Ireland, Michael Soden, suggested it was time for a merger between the two large Irish banks to create a 'super-bank' with an international presence as the best hope for the long-term viability of the Irish economy. If AIB were to be controlled from outside, it wouldn't be long before other financial institutions, including Bank of Ireland, would face a similar fate. 'If one bank goes they will all go, and that would not be good for the Irish economy,' he said.

Soden's views were based on his experience during six years at National Australia Bank. While in Sydney he had responsibility for the bank's operations in New Zealand, an economy that saw all its banks slip into foreign ownership over a seven-year period. He believed this has had a disastrous effect on the New Zealand economy and warned that the same could happen in Ireland. 'If the decisions on whether to allocate resources in Ireland are being made in Rome or Brussels, I am not sure we would be very high up on their agenda. They would simply go into areas that reflect their own desires,' he said.

Soden's suggestion got a cool reaction. A 'super-bank' would mean less competition with inflated fees, and a merger could mean the closure of hundreds of bank branches around the country and the loss of about 5,000 banking jobs, according to the Irish Bank Officials' Association. Even when in competition, AIB and Bank of Ireland had been accused of operating a cosy cartel at the expense of customers. It took the arrival of English and Scottish banks in the Republic to inject some real competition into Irish banking. Bank of Scotland forced AIB and Bank of Ireland to lower mortgage rates to match its more attractive products and was creating more competition for Irish consumers. AIB refused to comment on the merger speculation. Quinn said he could speak for or against the proposition if asked, but thought it unlikely that other EU states such as France would allow all of its banks to end up in foreign hands.

In the meantime AIB had to deal with the consequences of the Allfirst debacle. They would not go bust like Barings. But there were other examples that pointed to what might happen. When the trading divisions of the UK's National Westminster Bank, NatWest Markets, discovered a £90 million hole in its options-trading division in 1997, the head of NatWest Markets, Martin Owen, was ousted, the bank pulled back from investment banking, and ultimately exited that industry. NatWest was so badly wounded that it was later taken over by Royal Bank of Scotland. Similarly, when a Morgan Grenfell Asset Management fund manager incurred large losses, the parent, Deutsche Bank, simply absorbed the losses and re-branded the business as Deutsche Asset Management.

AIB could meet the losses at Baltimore from the 2001 profits. It had closed down proprietary currency trading at Allfirst. But the bank had been destabilised, and the question still had to be answered: whose heads, if any, should roll.

That would largely depend upon what Eugene Ludwig had been able to find out.

15
Pure Hollywood

The boards of Allied Irish Banks and Allfirst were called together at the AIB headquarters in Dublin on Tuesday 12 March to hear the findings of Eugene Ludwig's investigation of the trading fraud at Baltimore.

The Americans flew into Dublin and checked into the five-star Four Seasons hotel across the busy Merrion Road from AIB's headquarters. Security guards with earphones hovered around the lobby as the directors signed in, among them the former American ambassador to Ireland, Margaret Heckler. At 8.30 next morning limousines were waiting to take them the few hundred yards to AIB headquarters so that they would not have to encounter journalists or the Irish weather.

Susan Keating arrived in AIB headquarters immaculately groomed. When the lift opened onto the executive fourth floor she flashed a huge smile at everyone, kissed proffered cheeks and proceeded purposefully towards the pink-carpeted boardroom. One insider described it as 'pure Hollywood'.

The Allfirst president and chief executive had been there at least once before as a member of AIB's powerful group executive committee – she had been invited to join the executive committee in part as a way of involving her more in AIB management, and to give AIB more influence in its American subsidiary, which had a history of independence, indifference and sometimes confrontation with Dublin. On that occasion she had got a warm welcome and had been written-up as the first woman to reach such a height in Irish banking. This time the reception was much more formal, more devastatingly polite.

The main item on the agenda for the board meetings was the consideration of Ludwig's findings. Everyone knew that another item was blood-letting. It was evident there would be firings of those immediately responsible for the trading debacle, but the futures of Lochlann Quinn and Michael Buckley at the head of AIB, and Frank Bramble and Susan Keating in Allfirst were by no means assured. The media speculation about Susan Keating's future had been so intense, some of it citing AIB sources, that it seemed she had been set up for execution.

During the morning the twenty-nine men and women listened to Ludwig as he detailed the wide-scale lapses in controls that had allowed Rusnak to conceal his trading losses for five years. He pointed out the many red flags – enough, as someone noted, to decorate downtown Moscow – that were overlooked because Rusnak's two superiors 'missed the big picture'.

The 57-page report gave a detailed account of how an 'unusually clever and devious' trader had accumulated losses of $691.2 million before he was caught. It listed 89 reasons 'why the loss was not uncovered and why it was able to grow.' David Cronin, the executive vice-president of Allfirst and head of the treasury department was the 'key weak link in the control process.' However, management of both banks had failed in several respects.

'The senior management teams at both AIB and Allfirst should have insisted on much more rigorous risk assessment and audit reviews' of Rusnak's trading, said Ludwig. Proprietary trading activities 'are an extremely high risk activity no matter how small the activity appears to those in the senior levels of a bank's organisation.' Rusnak's losses were not discovered, he said, because AIB Group Risk, AIB and Allfirst senior management groups and the respective boards assumed that the control and audit procedures at Allfirst were 'sufficiently robust'. AIB appeared 'to have placed far too much reliance on the structures in place at Allfirst and on the reliability of Mr Cronin.' AIB knew that Cronin was the only person in Baltimore with the experience to monitor proprietary trading, but no proactive measures were taken in Dublin to actively monitor treasury policies and procedures. Neither the Allfirst Assets and Liabilities Committee which Cronin chaired, or AIB Group's market strategy committee, of which he was a member, appeared to have engaged in any rigorous examination of his conduct in supervising foreign exchange activity. Nor did AIB senior managers, risk managers or group ALCO in Dublin or their counterparts in Baltimore 'appreciate the risks associated

with Mr Rusnak's hedge fund style of foreign trading.' Even in the
absence of any sign of fraudulent conduct, 'the mere scope of Mr
Rusnak's trading activities and the size of the positions he was taking
warranted a much closer risk-management review.' The sheer size of
Mr Rusnak's positions and trading provided other opportunities for
Allfirst and AIB to examine Mr Rusnak's trading more closely,
Ludwig said, citing the occasion in March 2000 when Citibank
contacted AIB Group treasurer, Pat Ryan, about a $1 billion Rusnak
settlement, the only response being a request from Ryan to ask an
Allfirst official to make a 'discreet' inquiry. Ryan's direction con-
strained the Allfirst official, and 'no one at either bank followed up
with any inquiry as to why the offsetting gross Citibank positions
were so large.' AIB had also had other indications of the size of
Rusnak's trading from the filings made by Allfirst with the Securities
and Exchange Commission for 1999 and 2000 that clearly illustrated
that the notional value of foreign exchange trading at Allfirst was in
the billions of dollars, Ludwig said. There were AIB file notes prepared in 1997 by a manager of AIB's Strategic Assets and Liabilities
Management Committee, who reported to Ryan, that Allfirst's
average foreign exchange options book was $1 billion nominal. Also,
in February 2001 the AIB Group's financial reporting unit had raised
questions about the extent to which Rusnak was using the bank's
assets, and about the size of the cash flows generated by his activity.
Additionally, senior management in Baltimore and Dublin 'did
not focus sufficient attention on the Allfirst proprietary trading
operation'.

Everyone, it seemed, knew or should have known at some time or
other that Rusnak was doing big-time trading.

One reason for this lack of attention, Ludwig said, was that
Rusnak's operation was supposed to be small. His monthly stop-loss
was $200,000, the Value at Risk limit for all foreign exchange trading
was $2.5 million and the budgeted annual revenue for all foreign
exchange trading ran to only $1 million to $2 million. Another
reason was that Rusnak's trading was not part of Allfirst's core
business and was under the control of a well-regarded AIB senior
manager, David Cronin. And a third reason was that the data that
would have alerted senior management was altered by Rusnak to
mask the reports senior management received.

Much of the weight of Ludwig's censure fell upon the Allfirst treasury operation headed by Cronin. This consisted of three departments with a total staff of forty: the front office headed by treasury funds manager Robert Ray, in which Rusnak was a 'managing director', the middle office responsible for asset and liability management and risk control, and the back office responsible for confirming trades.

The very architecture of Allfirst's trading was flawed, Ludwig said. The trading had essentially become a hedge-fund operation but 'one lone trader in Baltimore' had no competitive advantage in that highly competitive and sophisticated market.

Rusnak was able to 'devise devious ways to obscure his position and profit and loss.' He took advantage of weak and inexperienced employees, some of whom were poorly trained, poorly supervised or lazy. Cronin believed him to be fundamentally a person of good character. When required, Rusnak bullied those who questioned him. His activities might have been facilitated by individuals at other firms, but Ludwig said he had not sufficient time 'to delve into that area'.

Specifically, he said, no one questioned why option counterparties repeatedly did not exercise profitable option transactions, no one questioned why two identical options with different expiry dates would have the same premia, no one questioned with senior management the large gross foreign exchange activity, and no one reviewed the large daily P/L (profit and loss) swings. Some personnel were careless, confirmation of trades was haphazard and very badly managed and executed, broker bills were not reconciled, there was no validation of counterparty details, there were instances of password sharing, and Rusnak's telephone calls were not recorded. Repeated breaches of limits were not properly followed up. Rusnak was allowed to trade on vacation even though banks in the US were required to bar traders from trading for two weeks a year. Nor was his after-hours trading verified.

Ludwig accused Cronin and Ray of missing the big picture. Ray 'inexplicably ignored numerous warning signs of Mr Rusnak's activity.' Given his limits, Rusnak's gross positions, level of daily turnover and the excessive attention paid to him by brokers should have alerted them. Even if Rusnak's hedge strategy existed, the basic risk on the visible gross size of the positions would have produced profit and loss swings many times greater than Rusnak's stop-loss limits. 'Mr Ray should not have missed this obvious point.'

No specific criticisms were made in the report of either bank's chairman or chief executive, though it left it open as to whether Bramble or the head of risk assessment and inveterate note-taker, Brian King, was telling the truth in two disputed episodes.

In conclusion, Ludwig said, he and his team 'have no definite basis to conclude at this point that anyone within Allfirst treasury other than Mr Rusnak had actual knowledge that Mr Rusnak was engaged in fraudulent or improper trading activity before the events leading up to the discovery of the fraud in February 2002.' They found no indication 'that anyone at AIB or Allfirst, outside of the Allfirst treasury group, were involved in, or had any knowledge that, fraudulent or improper trading activity was occurring at Allfirst, before the discovery of the fraud.' Nor had there been any effort of which they were aware by senior AIB or Allfirst personnel 'to conceal or cover up the facts.'

It was obvious to the members of the two boards that Cronin, Ray and several other more junior Allfirst officials would have to be sacked or, as Ludwig so delicately put it in his recommendations, new people should be found for their jobs. These were Cronin, Ray, back office clerk Larry Smith, head of internal audit Michael Husich, his colleague Lou Slifker, and Jan Palmer, senior vice-president of treasury operations administration. There were no differences between the two boards about this. However, with losses of such magnitude the question of responsibility at the very top could not be avoided.

The two boards separated to deliberate on Ludwig's conclusions. Allfirst directors filed out of the boardroom to an adjoining conference room.

Michael Buckley had good reason to feel that his position had strengthened since the news of the fraud broke. Many commentators, in Ireland and abroad, had cast doubts on his leadership, especially since he had had to admit just before the joint board meeting that as far back as May 2001 he had been told of a market rumour of excessive trading in Allfirst but had done no more than ask for and accept an explanation from Cronin that, as Ludwig put it, 'satisfied AIB'.

The AIB chief executive had set out first to assuage unease among AIB staff. Many AIB employees would have been suspicious about Buckley because he had come from the Capital Markets division, which would be considered a very anti-trade-union environment. He was not a career banker with roots in the old Munster & Leinster power base. On 6 February he had sent an e-mail to bank officials across the AIB Group to rally support: 'I can well imagine the anger of all of you who work hard every day to meet profits and cost goals on hearing of the $750 million loss. It is a heavy blow for us to take. But we will survive and recover from this unprecedented situation,' he wrote. 'You will have many questions about the situation. I will do all I can to get answers for you but you will understand that there are some subjects that I just can't cover at this point. Please e-mail, fax or mail questions to me at the addresses below. If you wish, you don't have to give your name. When I have more news I will write again.'

His e-mail resulted in a flurry of what one AIB staff member called 'sympathy cards', with signatures, offering supportive comments and telling Buckley how unfairly he was being treated by the media. From Cork came several tributes along the lines of, 'We're all in it together.'

Buckley sent another staff e-mail on 12 February. One of the concerns he encountered in responses to his first message was payment of annual bonuses. Profit-sharing and bonuses would come up for review by the AIB board 'in a fair and business-like way,' he promised. (Bonuses for senior executives were later cancelled.)

One of Buckley's own concerns was the pounding he was taking in the media. 'Many of you will no doubt face comments, good and bad, from people who will find it hard to separate fact from fiction in the blizzard of media reports,' he wrote. 'The next week or so won't be easy. In this period, while we are awaiting the Ludwig report, we can expect, as is already the case, that the stories will be based on "facts" that are simply not true and will make allegations that have no foundation.'

The bank's investor relations team had meanwhile been canvassing AIB's major investors about their confidence, or lack of it, in the bank's leadership. Goodbody Stockbrokers, Merrill Lynch, and Salomon Smith Barney stockbrokers helped ascertain the views of AIB shareholders. The message coming back was that, with some exceptions, investors felt that getting rid of the AIB chief executive might not be in their best interest. The share price had recovered and the pressure had eased.

But the pressure had not eased on Susan Keating since her arrival in Dublin. There was a strong feeling in the AIB boardroom that she should acknowledge her responsibilities and resign. The fraud had happened on her watch, in a bank that had been under-performing and where the controls were corrupt. 'There was a total breakdown here,' said an AIB source. 'Any bank chief executive would look first thing in the morning at the activity reports from the risk areas of the bank, especially currency trading and interest rates. That this was going on without Keating being told or asking about the trading is incredible.' It wasn't just a question of a rogue trader but of failed corporate governance. Bramble and Keating were already convinced that there had been an orchestrated campaign in the media by supporters of AIB management for their dismissals to assuage investor anger.

In the room where Allfirst directors met separately to the AIB directors in the main boardroom, resistance built up against any pre-emptory dumping of Keating. The Allfirst chief executive had the backing of most of her co-directors. Bramble was on her side; they went back a long way together, to their days in the failed MNC bank. Jerry Casey and Bramble had brought in six of the other directors who would be sympathetic: Sherry Bellamy, the vice-president and general counsel of Verizon Communications; James Brady, managing director (mid-Atlantic) of Ballantree International; Margaret Heckler, former US ambassador to Ireland; William Kirchhoff, vice-chairman of Cleveland Brothers Equipment Company; Andrew Maier, a private investor; and Morton Rapoport, president and chief executive of the University of Maryland Medical System.

Bramble, AIB's highest-paid executive, said that he had already decided he was stepping down and retiring from the bank. He had made his mind up before the scandal, he said. As chief executive or chairman for all the five years while the fraud was being perpetrated, his departure would inevitably be linked in the public mind with the Rusnak debacle. It was sacrifice enough for the Baltimore bank.

The two groups broke for lunch. Platters of cold cuts and seafood were provided. No wine was produced from AIB's well-stocked cellar. Then it was back to separate deliberations. The two boards communicated through Gary Kennedy. Throughout the afternoon and evening Kennedy shuttled between the two rooms.

One of the strongest arguments from the Keating camp for her survival was that when a market source told Buckley about reports of heavy trading in Baltimore in May 2001, the AIB chief executive, who was also a member of the Allfirst board, had not communicated this extraordinary tip to her. Some of the sixteen directors were prepared to accept a measure of responsibility for the fraud but did not want to let Buckley entirely off the hook.

The Allfirst side also had another plausible defence: their inability to fully control the treasury because of the unique reporting relationship dating back to 1989 when AIB inserted Cronin into the Baltimore bank's senior management team. His arrival was not well received and he was viewed, in Cronin's words, as the 'home office spy' and shut out from management meetings. After Bramble became chief executive, Cronin said that he was treated with more openness and collegiality. But he had a *de jure* and only partly *de facto* reporting relationship with the management in Baltimore. Cronin's budget, salary and bonus were controlled by the bank where he worked, but he was required to apply AIB policy to the treasury operation and he maintained an informal network of former home office colleagues with whom he discussed business. His files and telephone records showed that he kept up a close and constant contact with Pat Ryan. Ludwig had recorded that Bramble and Keating harboured concerns about Cronin but were of the view that Buckley and other AIB senior executives would protect the former AIB man from Cork. On several occasions Bramble had asked that Cronin's reporting relationship be changed so that he could be more closely supervised or removed. When Keating became chief executive in January 2001 she raised the possibility of having Cronin report to a new chief financial officer who could more closely monitor his activities. Ludwig had concluded that while 'senior officers of AIB also recognised that the Allfirst's treasurer's level of energy and commitment were lower than expected, they nevertheless continued to believe that he was the best person for the job.'

In the AIB boardroom, the most dramatic moment came when Buckley and Quinn offered their resignations. They left the boardroom to allow their offer to be discussed. John McGuckian took the chair. The directors rejected their offer and the two men returned to the boardroom.

It was not an attempt at grandstanding but a reflection of accountability, said Buckley afterwards. 'I tendered it on a belief that, when
you look at accountability, that you can't stop at any particular level
in a company. The buck, as far as I was concerned, stopped with me.'
He added that, 'it took a bit of persuading' by the board to convince
him to stay on in the job. Quinn said that as chairman of the bank
he had a responsibility to ensure the quality of management at AIB.
'The board's general view was that less damage would be done to the
bank if I stayed. I hope they are correct.'

The melodrama in the AIB boardroom did not embarrass Keating
into doing the same. The 'Velvet Hammer' did not subject herself to
a similar vote by offering her resignation. 'It did not make financial
sense to quit,' said a former colleague. 'But if they force her to leave,
she gets a big severance package.' The three AIB directors on the
Allfirst board, Buckley, Kennedy and Mulcahy, held all the votes
by virtue of AIB's ownership of Allfirst stock. They would win any
division in the Allfirst board if it came to that. But they would need
a majority of the Allfirst directors on this issue to obtain a credible
result. 'Jerry Casey, no friend of Buckley and his growing interference
at Allfirst, marshalled the Allfirst board with the assistance of
Bramble and Keating,' according to one insider. As darkness fell over
Dublin Bay behind AIB headquarters, the Allfirst directors did the
unthinkable. They let AIB directors know that, at a push, they
would offer their resignations if AIB attempted to remove Keating.

Suddenly Quinn and Buckley had a possible mutiny on their
hands. If the American directors resigned, the Baltimore bank would
be left rudderless. It would lose more credibility in the mid-Atlantic
region where it operated. It would be a disaster. AIB did not press the
matter to confrontation. Keating survived.

But the Allfirst board suffered two more casualties. Jerry Casey
and former AIB chief executive, Tom Mulcahy, stood down from
their long-standing directorships to make way for two non-executive
directors with recognised skills in the financial services sector. 'The
board ambushed Buckley with an ultimatum that if Keating was fired
they would resign *en masse*, resulting in total turmoil,' according to
the insider. 'In the horse-trading that followed, Buckley and chairman Quinn secured the resignations of Casey and Mulcahy.'

This was a big break with the past. Casey, when chairman of the

Baltimore bank in 1994, and Mulcahy, then AIB chief executive, had engineered the coup that ousted Charlie Cole from the chief executive's office at Allfirst, then called First Maryland, giving Casey a free hand to bring in a new team that would show him a level of respect and deference he did not get from the First Maryland old guard. But things had not worked out. An important part of the bank's operation had become dysfunctional. Mulcahy had been AIB's chief executive for most of the five-year period when the losses occurred and was now chairman of Aer Lingus and had an enormous burden trying to turn around the troubled national carrier.

As far as the Baltimore board was concerned they had now offered up three high profile casualties. AIB had produced none, though Pat Ryan's retirement which had been announced in January would now go ahead. Not a single AIB executive had been made to take the consequences. Bramble and Keating were furious. 'At the end of the day, the whole thing was a mess, and it was very difficult to apportion blame,' said AIB director, Padraic Fallon, later. 'There wasn't anyone at a senior position in the group whom we could fire, that was the really frustrating thing.'

The meetings broke up after 11 pm. They agreed to reconvene the following morning to confirm their decisions and hold a press conference the day after. On the way out Keating was as ever poised and assured. She kissed her would-be executioners on the cheek as she headed for the waiting limousine.

Next morning at breakfast, security was even tighter in the hotel. When Allfirst directors met for a late breakfast in the dining room, security guards kept everyone else out. Later that day Keating and Bramble were spotted behind the tinted windows of a limousine heading from the Four Seasons to the airport. They did not talk to reporters before leaving. When she arrived back in Baltimore Keating was, despite her triumph, said to be in a furious mood.

The AIB board still had to decide whether to release the Ludwig report in full or prepare an executive summary for publication. Quinn was against releasing it in full. 'You are not getting it,' he had told the Irish Times before the joint board meeting. 'If Ludwig was to write this report knowing it was going to be published, I think it might cramp his style. It is a confidential report for the board.' However it was likely that details of Rusnak's activities and the role of others would eventually be made public in the US. The board decided to let it all be made public and gain credit for transparency rather than see details dragged into the public domain bit by bit over the next few months.

The AIB directors also had to decide the level of Bramble's compensation. He was the highest-paid executive in the AIB Group network, receiving an annual salary of $725,000 plus bonus and other compensations. His package was worth €1.7 million the previous year. A formula was worked out and left to the lawyers to finalise. He would receive a lump sum in lieu of his pension. He was entitled to a pension equalling an average of 60 per cent of the three highest wage-earning years of his career and that worked out at $2.9 million. The bank would also make clear that he had decided to leave before the trading losses were uncovered and not because of the fraud. The board remuneration committee of Quinn, Adrian Burke, Derek Higgs and John McGuckian also had to decide whether to cancel all bonuses across AIB or confine this penalty to the top echelons and staff at Allfirst.

The audit committee also had some hard soul-searching to do. Its chairman, Adrian Burke, would have to convene with Higgs, Dermot Gleeson, Don Godson and Mike Sullivan to review and improve its effectiveness in the light of the failings Ludwig had reported. The relationship with PricewaterhouseCoopers, the long-standing auditors of both AIB and Allfirst, would also have to be examined. Some board members at Allfirst had been vitriolic about the failure of the accountants to identify the treasury fraud.

The priority for the board now was to show that it had acted decisively and responsibly in response to this crisis and that investors could be satisfied that no further shocks or upsets would materialise. The blame had been laid on six staff plus Rusnak at its small treasury outpost in Baltimore. None had got any severance. Cronin, the person who had tried to have the treasury operation integrated with Dublin some years back, was to take the fall and to be publicly excoriated.

Some AIB staff members felt it was unfair to link Pat Ryan's retirement with the affair and that he had got a raw deal. He had been implicitly criticised in the report over the Citibank query whereas the report did not hint at any censure of Buckley over his handling of the markets tip in May 2001. This was something that had troubled some people inside AIB itself. 'In AIB if a rumour reached head office that a manager in one town was lending too much money or the manager in another was drinking every night, a hit team would be sent out to take the place apart,' said an AIB source. 'In a business as dangerous as forex (foreign exchange), when you get a market rumour every red light comes on.' The relationship between the AIB chief and the group treasurer, known as the father figure of the Irish money markets, had never been very close. Ryan had been head of treasury at AIB capital markets when Buckley arrived from NCB. He was favourite to succeed Mulcahy as the division's head. He was out-manoeuvered and Buckley got the job. By the time Buckley became chief executive in 2001, Ryan had already decided to retire. The group treasurer had dropped off the Group Executive Committee and was preparing to depart when Buckley sent him to Baltimore to investigate Rusnak's trading.

Details of those departing the bank, including Ryan, appeared in some newspapers the next morning ahead of the press conference to present the Ludwig report. Many bank staff learned of the outcome when they bought their *Irish Times* on the way to work.

Buckley sent an apologetic e-mail to bank staff: 'This was a leak which did not come from me or from our media relations/communications team who have been superb throughout this crisis. I can tell you I was as annoyed as some of you were that this happened.' He wrote that 'Both boards agreed that where the report found people to be culpable, they would be dismissed. They were determined that wider accountabilities would be identified on a person-by-person basis, up to the top, and that appropriate action would be taken. Each case was extensively discussed. I did not feel that I should be exempt from this process, nor did the chairman. We both put our resignations on the table and asked the AIB board to determine, without our participation, whether either of the resignations should be accepted in order to underpin the credibility of our company. I believe that the boards' discussions were rigorous and taken together provide a solid and credible basis for moving forward to the next phase of rebuilding the damage we have suffered.' The newspapers would continue with intensive coverage for some time yet 'and some of what they say will continue to be unfair. We will just have to put up with that,' he stated.

'The fact that Susan Keating is to remain CEO of Allfirst has pro-
voked much discussion. The remarks made by our chairman,
Lochlann Quinn, are relevant here. He said that the board carefully
reviewed the broader accountability of those individuals in the
reporting line up from David Cronin, both in Allfirst and in AIB
Group, including the chairman and myself. The board decided that
it would be wrong to hold Susan responsible for the fraud for two
main reasons. The first is that she only assumed responsibility for the
Allfirst treasury operations at the beginning of 2001. Secondly, the
Ludwig report concludes that she was justified in having confidence
in the Allfirst treasurer whose competence in treasury was unques-
tioned in both AIB and Allfirst.'

Keating and the new Allfirst chairman had 'a big challenge ahead
of them. They need all the support they can get to move our retail
and commercial franchise in Maryland, south central Pennsylvania
and the DC area to a new level of performance. I will be supporting
them in every way in their efforts. It is vital for all our sakes that they
and all our colleagues in Allfirst are successful.' He reminded
employees that they were all 'guardians' of AIB's reputation. 'If you
have any concerns or issues I genuinely would like to hear them.'

Ludwig's report was delivered to the Dublin Stock Exchange at
7.00 am after the fourteen-hour joint board meeting. Before leaving
Dublin to fly back to Washington, he told a *Baltimore Sun* reporter,
'It was as much a set of human tragedies as I've ever seen. There was
a human dynamic here that was unholy.' Rusnak lost money the old
fashioned way: 'He bet wrong.' He supported the decision to keep
Keating in her job. 'I don't want to be an apologist for her but it is
responsible of the board in this case not to take her out.' Cronin and
Ray were 'not crooked' he added. 'They relied on the outward signs
of an inward grace.' He had learned something himself, he said. 'To
be a really good banker you've got to be sceptical.'

The survival of Keating was greeted with amazement by many
commentators and investors. A spokesman for the National
Association of Pension Funds in Britain said, 'If she did know
what was happening, then clearly she should go. If she didn't, she
should still go because she ought to have had a better knowledge of
what was going on within her organisation.' Analyst Jonathan
Gollins of the Bank of America – which made huge profits from

Rusnak – said, 'I don't think this restores any confidence in incumbent management.'

There were some advantages to be gained by Keating staying on which AIB could play up, such as the need for stability. She could also be effectively sidelined. The AIB board replaced Bramble with Eugene Sheehy, one of Buckley's closest associates. A senior AIB source said nonchalantly: 'She's history. It's not personal. If you blow it you go. It's only a matter of finding a formula now.'

16
Banana Skins

Nick Leeson woke early on the morning of 6 February 2002. He switched on his television and flicked through the channels. An item on Bloomberg caught his attention. 'I was looking at it because there was nothing on TV. It came up as breaking news, the story had just hit the news wires,' he said. As he watched the news of John Rusnak's trading debacle unfold the phone began to ring. 'A few people called to see where I was, making sure I wasn't in America, just messing around,' Leeson said.

The man who broke Barings Bank through his rogue trading in Singapore was interviewed throughout the day on UK and international news bulletins. His picture made the front pages of the British evening papers as the media sought to explain what appeared to be an identical financial disaster.

'It was akin to being on the run again,' he said. 'My story had already finished but I was being associated with this once more. It's a bit strange getting on a tube in London where everybody is reading the *Evening Standard* and to see yourself on the front page. I just kept my head down and tried not to draw any attention to myself. A few people did recognise me. I got a few looks and some people were whispering but in general people are quite respectful.'

Since then Leeson has closely examined the Allfirst fraud. If he were to use it as a case study for a conference, his conclusion would be that the fraud happened because the controls were not good enough, he said. He also believes that those in charge of Rusnak didn't understand the options and other financial instruments he was using, and as a result could not spot the warning signs on the bank's balance sheet.

'You have to wonder why nobody ever asked very basic questions. There were very basic checks that should have been carried out. It was kindergarten stuff.'

AIB might have saved many hundreds of millions of dollars had any of their treasury staff, in Dublin or Baltimore, attended one of Leeson's risk management conferences. The man who knew best how to subvert the controls and to weave a web of deceit to cover his tracks as a loss-making trader now made a living by sharing his expertise with financial institutions. The poacher-turned-gamekeeper wasn't that surprised that another big-time rogue trader had emerged who one day might compete for his business. Banks never learn from mistakes, he said. 'There are risk management surveys done every year. After Barings the presence of a rogue trader was the third-highest concern amongst financial institutions. By the time Allfirst came around it had moved down to number twenty-three or twenty-four. Banks forget all too easily.'

Leeson was referring to the annual 'Banana Skins' report of the Centre for the Study of Financial Innovation in London, a survey of risks in banking sponsored by PricewaterhouseCoopers and based on a poll of top bankers, regulators and analysts from fifteen countries. Rogue trading was ranked 24th in a list of 30 potential risks in the survey for 2001. It was published on 6 February, the day the news of Rusnak's losses at Allfirst broke. With rather bad timing, the Centre's director, David Lascelles, wrote in the report: 'Some banana skins come and go. Some are hardy perennials. The rogue trader, so troublesome in 1996 and 1997, has completely disappeared.'

Losses were practically inevitable when banks engaged in proprietary trading, but within a controlled environment the cost to the banks of bad calls on currency movements could be contained. Financial institutions rarely publicised these losses. They would take it on the chin, fire the trader and hope the press didn't get wind of it.

'The trader goes on to work for another bank,' said Leeson. 'There are no really bad implications for the trader. It's all about attracting as little attention as possible.'

Leeson claimed that conjuring up fictitious deals if a mistake occurred was a widespread practice that happened every day in the broking world. Mistakes could be commonplace in the dealing room. Somebody might misunderstand a hand signal and buy the wrong amount of currency.

At Barings, any errors that couldn't be rectified in the Singapore operation were transferred to London and put into an error account numbered 99905 where they would be reconciled. On a busy day Leeson might have made fifty such entries into that account. These would then have to be systematically accounted for in London. The bank suggested this was becoming tedious, and worried that the high volume of transactions could invite closer scrutiny from the auditors. It was suggested to Leeson that he should create an error account in Singapore to streamline the process. The account had to be assigned a five-digit number. Eight was a lucky Chinese number, so Leeson settled on 88888. He needed all the luck he could handle, he told his settlements clerk.

A few weeks later London decided to revert to the status quo. Errors were again to be booked through to head office. The 88888 account should have been closed and wiped from the bank's system, but it lay dormant. This account then provided the vehicle for Leeson to cover up his massive losses without attracting attention.

He first used it to conceal a £20,000 trading error made by a very junior trader. Leeson was operating on a shoe-string in Singapore. Barings would not allow him to hire any more traders and costs were being cut to the bone. The trader, Kim Wong, was to buy twenty futures contracts for Fuji Bank for the Nikkei-225 Index that was traded on the Tokyo Stock Exchange. The contracts entitled the holders to buy or sell a basket of shares quoted on the Nikkei at a set price in the future, usually at the end of March, June, September and December. The owner of the contract paid a small up-front payment or margin when it was purchased. Wong had been hired on a salary of £4,000 a year and was very inexperienced. Amidst the frenetic trading she got confused and sold twenty Nikkei contracts for Fuji Bank instead of buying them. When the markets re-opened the following week Barings would have to buy twenty contracts for Fuji Bank and would also have to reverse the wrong deal booked by the trader. Leeson estimated this would cost £20,000.

On Monday Leeson reactivated the 88888 error account and booked a fictitious trade showing that Fuji Bank had bought twenty contracts. He also amended Friday's daily trading sheet to show that Fuji needed to be made good for the contracts at the price they had directed Barings to buy them. The trade would look normal, but because this deal had never actually taken place Leeson also had to make an opposite trade that would reconcile that part of the transaction, and book that too into the 88888 account. As far as Barings was concerned Fuji had bought twenty contracts at the original price it had wanted, the error account had sold the same twenty contracts at the same price to balance that, and the real sale of the contracts that Wong had put through was also entered in the 88888 account.

It was precisely the sort of activity which Rusnak was to engage in at Allfirst treasury. Leeson contended that for all of these reasons it was 'widespread practice' to conjure up fictitious deals if an error took place, and then solve the problem internally. 'It happens every day in the broking world.'

'The rewriting of these trades was invisible to the Singapore International Monetary Exchange (SIMEX) because the original sale was now in the 88888 account,' so everything tallied with their records, he explained in *Rogue Trader*, the story of his experiences published in 1996. This exercise bought him some time to sort the mess out.

Leeson's strength was as a currency trader and he had little knowledge of trading contracts based on the movements of stock markets. He was aware from other colleagues, however, that it was generally very difficult to rectify these mistakes. The trader couldn't simply go to the customer, give them the contract to buy the stock at a higher price, and reimburse the additional cost. It was highly complex. In this case Fuji Bank would have entered the contract details, including the purchase price it had directed Barings to pay, into its own computer system. It would use this information to work out how much tax it would have to pay on the transaction. The performance of share movements in the future would also be tracked from the specified purchase price. To supply a contract at a different price would distort all of these calculations. It would also upset the calculations that would have been made to assess how Fuji should hedge these contracts or take action to compensate for any loss if the Nikkei moved in the opposite direction. On top of this it would have been highly unprofessional to have to go back to the client and admit to this mistake.

Despite his best efforts to protect the trader, Wong resigned, saying she could not cope with the pressure. If Leeson had fired her immediately he could have written off the relatively small £20,000 loss. Three days later the cost of the bad trade had tripled from £20,000 to £60,000. It was now too big to disclose to his superiors and would only raise more questions as to why he had waited so long to confront the problem.

The £60,000 loss was also buried in the 88888 account. Over the next few months, up to the end of 1992, Leeson put thirty errors into that account, including particularly large ones that he thought would otherwise get his newly-recruited traders into trouble. The 88888 account was legitimate, but the mistakes were getting bigger. If at the end of the month when the trading assets and liabilities were reviewed and a large unapproved loss suddenly materialised, Leeson would have lost his job.

Leeson, the son of a plasterer from Watford, had worked his way up at Barings to become the bank's leading foreign exchange trader. By 1993, he had made more than £10 million on the books – about 10 per cent of Barings' total profit for that year.

Near the time of year when Barings calculated the bonuses to be paid to its traders, one of Leeson's colleagues, George Seow, made a really big error. Seow bought rather than sold one hundred contracts worth around £8 million. The mistake was big enough to have Seow sacked on the spot, the operation closed down and bonuses cancelled. Barings had a policy of paying almost half of its pre-tax profits in staff bonuses. This would represent the biggest portion of the traders' annual compensation.

The transaction was concealed in the swelling 88888 account to safeguard their bonuses. He now needed a huge amount of cash to trade out of the mess. Leeson was confident he could find some excuse to have funds transferred from London but suddenly he had a better idea. He would sell an option to buy yen to another financial institution. It would pay an initial premium on the contract and Leeson would use that money to cancel some of the deficit in the 88888 account. The remainder would have to come from London, he reasoned. His London office was as gullible as the treasury in Allfirst. His luck began to run out when the economic impact of the 18 January 1995 earthquake in Kobe, Japan, depressed the markets. By autumn of that year his total losses amounted to £208 million.

When asked why he never came clean and ended the nightmare, he still finds it hard to give a definitive answer. 'I have been asked that question so many times and I still find it difficult to answer. You start off with small steps, baby steps. At that stage you are always trying to rationalise what you are doing. You are trading, but you are only trying to get the money back, not to make a profit. In the beginning I was expecting a rap on the knuckles for my losses but didn't believe I would be sacked. Then as they grew I knew that was the natural outcome.' You just simply live with it, he said. 'You have the reality of what is going on at work. You are living a lie while living your life with your friends and family, and you keep going to keep that lie going. You don't want to let them down. They are the people you find it most difficult to be honest with. It's difficult to tell them you are not doing well. They think everything has been built on a firm foundation but in fact the house of cards is about to tumble.'

When Barings' internal audit team began to close in on Leeson in early 1995, he resorted to forging documents to stay ahead. 'Falsifying documents is a big leap. You are moving into the criminal phase,' he said.

When Barings' financial controller called to request that he provide confirmation of a purchase of 7.78 billion yen from Spear, Leeds & Kellogg, Leeson took letters that confirmed previous deals, made blank copies and reproduced the signatures of the SLK managing director and the head of Barings' financial products group. Photocopying proved to be the most difficult task and he spent over an hour trying to get the letters to look normal. He then went home and faxed the two forged letters to himself at Barings.

Rusnak used a variation of the same trick when he rented a post box in New York and forged a confirmation on his PC which he then had posted from New York to the bank's independent auditors.

Leeson's requests for extra funds to continue his trading activities ultimately aroused suspicion. The bank ordered a spot audit at Singapore where it found that his losses came to more than £800 million.

Leeson went on the run, moving through resorts in Malaysia with his wife, Lisa, and finding out the final consequences of his actions when he saw a headline in the *New Straits Times*: 'British Merchant Bank Collapse'. When he tried to return to London a few days later to face the music he was apprehended *en route* at Frankfurt. He lost a battle to be tried in the United Kingdom and was extradited to

Singapore where in December 1995 he was sentenced to six-and-a-half years after pleading guilty to two charges of deceiving the auditors of Barings in a way 'likely to cause harm to their reputation' and to cheating the Singapore International Monetary Exchange.

'The loss of your liberty is frightening,' said Leeson, looking back at his time in prison. 'You have to try to come to terms with it, hope you will be strong enough to come through it. Rusnak will have to face up to what he has done. Prison is a tough place. You meet a lot of scary people. Coming from a white-collar environment, you have never experienced anything like it, and never expected to. You are scared. You have to find your feet. That takes time.'

While he was detained in Germany, his wife visited him every week. 'She piggy-backed me through. In Singapore, it was a much tougher regime. I spent up to twenty-three hours alone every day for two years. During that time you do a lot of soul-searching. You have to find something to motivate yourself. For me there was a perverse sense of relief when I knew what the sentence was. There had been huge speculation. It's terrible not knowing what it is.' The British press had suggested he could face twenty-one years in prison.

'I cried every week, sometimes I cried for days and weeks on end. You have got to get to know what your term of imprisonment will be as soon as possible. I had to work out how long I thought I could do. I had decided this was eight years. With standard remission it would have reduced to five. That was my threshold. I had told friends and family that if I got any longer than that then suicide was the only option. It takes some time to work out just what your limit is. Some days in Singapore I would look for the sharpest corner of the cell and get ready to run into it, to knock myself out. I would be hyper-ventilating at seven in the morning and I still had another three-and-a-half years to do. You just don't know how much you can cope with. Now I believe that what doesn't kill you will make you stronger.'

Leeson's marriage to Lisa broke up two-and-a-half years into his sentence. Leeson was hospitalised after suffering acute stomach pains and in August 1998 was diagnosed as having cancer of the colon. Four days later surgeons at Changi General Hospital removed a tumour and cut out part of his large intestine. Less than two weeks after undergoing chemotherapy treatment he was sent back to prison. The surgeons who operated on the rogue trader put his chances of survival over the following five years at 70 per cent, as the cancer had not spread from the colon to the lymph nodes. His application for early release on medical grounds was turned down. He was released in July 1999 with time off for good behaviour.

When he returned to Britain, Leeson found that he was still the subject of media attention. 'Barings is still a fascinating story. I get paid money to talk about it at dinner. I am also studying for a degree in psychology. I go into my final year in September [2002]. This will give me a different string to my bow, how I will use it has still to be determined,' he said.

'I get paid for talking about the most embarrassing episode in my life. I generally tell the story of what happened and there is usually a question and answer session at which people can ask about certain details. It's self-deprecating. I don't try to blame others. I don't want to look like a scapegoat. I also laugh about it. Laughter can be a great coping strategy.'

The after-dinner circuit together with risk-management conferences became Nick Leeson's means of livelihood. He also promoted a treasury magazine in the UK. He is entitled to only 50 per cent of his earnings; the remainder goes to those handling the liquidation of Barings. This arrangement would continue for as along as the legal actions taken against Barings' auditors, PricewaterhouseCoopers remained live.

Leeson was struck by the similarities between his activities and those of John Rusnak. 'As the story developed it seemed to be ninety-nine per cent similar to what I had done. The difference was that AIB was a strongly-capitalised bank and could withstand the loss.'

When the Rusnak trading losses were exposed, AIB sought to play down any similarities between what happened at Barings and at Allfirst, for fear of triggering a panic amongst its shareholders, customers and staff.

Leeson believed the problems that were endemic at Barings were also evident at AIB and Allfirst. 'I find that frightening. It means that the same levels of incompetence and negligence within the mid- and senior management of the bank were still there.'

In both cases, the traders falsified their real trading positions in the banks' accounting records. Leeson and Rusnak both created bogus trades that gave the appearance that their positions were hedged, giving their managers nothing untoward to worry about. The two traders worked frantically to trade their way out of their losses, but kept losing more money until they were eventually caught. Leeson lost £850 million, Rusnak $691 million.

Senior executives at Barings and AIB both heard market rumours about enormous trading that could have alerted them to a potential problem long before the traders were found out. In both cases these rumours were followed up. Leeson was able to reassure the bank that his positions were all covered and that there was very little downside for Barings from his trading activities. AIB chief executive, Michael Buckley, was assured by Allfirst treasurer, David Cronin, that there had been no unusually large transactions, it just appeared that way because of new trading arrangements with Citibank and Bank of America. Both Leeson and Rusnak were operating in outposts a long way from head office which were under constant pressure to keep costs down. Both had forceful personalities that allowed them to intimidate their colleagues from asking awkward questions.

Leeson noted how AIB swiftly put the spotlight firmly on Rusnak and Baltimore, deflecting the focus from Dublin. 'It was great for Michael Buckley and all of the executives to put the attention on one guy. They tried to localise it to Baltimore. They called it a devious and complex fraud. It may have been devious but it was not complex. People were not making the necessary checks. Where the buck stopped was questionable. Peter Norris, the chief executive of Barings, put his hand up when the fraud was discovered. The chiefs at AIB were not doing their jobs.'

From time to time Leeson ran into former Barings' employees at the events he attended, although they generally steered clear of him. 'Former colleagues you meet can be quite protective of Barings. They don't want to get into an argument with me because they know they will come off worse. If I am challenged by one of them when I am speaking I will explain a very specific episode to back up what I am saying, which they do not like. They know I know the level of their stupidity. All of my skeletons are out of the cupboard these days.'

Leeson said that he was a different person now and determined to get on and make a new life for himself. 'I will always wish it never happened but I am going to move on,' he said. 'I have learned a lot about myself. I react differently now to situations and I realise how strong you can be when you need to be. I will pay back as much money as I can but I am not going to spend the rest of my life saying sorry.'

17

The Sore Tooth

For months the scandal reverberated throughout AIB and Allfirst. Top executives lost their jobs or were reassigned. Reputations were shredded. Rusnak's contacts in another bank were fired. Millions were spent on the Ludwig inquiry and in follow up actions. Lawyers set their billing clocks as legal actions began. The future of AIB became a topic of national debate. The great Irish venture into American commercial banking teetered on the point of collapse.

Six weeks after the crisis broke, Eugene Sheehy arrived from Dublin to take over at Allfirst as executive chairman. The Carlow man had been managing director of AIB in the Republic of Ireland and a promoter of the bank's links with the Gaelic Athletic Association. Buckley gave him the title of executive chairman. It was carefully chosen. The word 'executive' clearly implied that unlike Bramble, who had earned the nickname 'Never There' because of his frequent absences, Sheehy would be around making executive-type decisions.

Frank Bramble left the bank soon after the boardroom theatrics in Dublin over what Eugene Ludwig called the 'fourth-largest bank fraud in history.' The MNC banker, brought in by Jerry Casey eight years earlier to help expand First Maryland through acquisitions, left on 30 April 2002 without collecting a bonus for his last year, but with a lump sum payment of $2.9 million in lieu of pension. There had been one major acquisition – that of Dauphin Deposit Bank in Harrisburg, Pennsylvania in 1997 – during his eight years as CEO and then chairman of AIB's American subsidiary. Bramble had not, however, achieved the goals he set for himself after that. He had said then that Allfirst was 'very interested' in expanding into West Virginia to the west, Virginia to the south, and New Jersey to the north. With an 'active acquisition strategy' it would be 'in the top three in all of the markets in our region.' But no more acquisitions had been made. Instead Allfirst's assets had fallen from $18.3 billion to $17.8 billion in the intervening three years.

Within a month of leaving Allfirst, Bramble was given a job by his old boss, Alfred Lerner, who had made him chief executive of MNC in 1991 just before the failing bank was sold to NationsBank. Lerner made him vice-chairman of a Wilmington-based subsidiary of his credit card company, MBNA. The chairman Charles M Cawley, a member of the board of the American Ireland fund and a prominent fundraiser for President George W Bush, welcomed Bramble to the company as 'a man with impeccable character.'

Brian King, 56, head of the risk assessment group, was the next senior player in the drama to depart. On 25 April the bank announced that the executive vice-president in charge of risk assessment would leave Allfirst to devote more time to charitable and other non-profit organisations. The news was greeted with some satisfaction by members of the pre-1994 old guard, who recalled how the former army helicopter pilot had sided with Jerry Casey before the ousting of Charlie Cole. The veteran of twenty-seven years had spent most of his career in human resources, and his late appointment to risk assessment had been much criticised internally because of his lack of experience in such a critical field. The press release referred to a plan announced the previous year to centralise some finance and risk functions in Dublin. His retirement 'coincides with the implementation of this plan.'

Susan Keating won the battle of Ballsbridge but she lost the war. In mid-July, four months after she survived Ludwig's scathing report about lack of controls in Baltimore, AIB announced that the 51-year-old banker from Los Angeles would leave her $675,000-a-year job as president and chief executive of Allfirst on 31 July 2002. She was the ninth person to step down, retire or be fired by the bank since the losses. Announcing her departure, Allfirst's new executive chairman, Eugene Sheehy, said, 'We agree on most issues but have debated some aspects of the best way forward for the company.' In bank-speak this was tantamount to saying they could not co-exist.

Philip Hosmer, the spokesman for Allfirst, depicted Keating's departure in terms appropriate to a divorce. There had been 'discussions and debates between Susan and Eugene and they came to a mutual separation,' he said. It was based on philosophical differences about the future direction of Allfirst that were 'strategic and long-term.'

AIB had not tried to persuade her to stay. Aside from the Rusnak scandal the bank had been underperforming. Allfirst slipped from 46th to 49th place in terms of total assets held by American banks between 1999 and 2001. After the scandal it fell to 55th place. In May 2002 it was ranked 147th among the top 150 commercial bank companies in the United States by return on assets the previous year. The bank's non-performing loans had increased by 7.38 per cent to $121.7 million.

Sheehy took over the positions of Allfirst president and chief executive. For the first time since the Irish arrived in Baltimore in 1983, an AIB executive was in the CEO's seat, and none of the three top jobs at Maryland's second-largest bank was held by an American banker.

It was the end of the era of the 'MNC mafia', whose arrival had resulted in the disbandment of the team of bankers under Charlie Cole, and had produced years of staff turmoil and turnover. (Charlie Cole had meantime become chairman and chief executive of Legg Mason Trust, part of a global financial services company located at Light Street, a block away from Allfirst headquarters, and, like First Maryland during Cole's time, a big sponsor of tennis in the region.)

It was the end too of Jerry Casey's role in the bank he had so painfully wrestled from Cole. The Cork banker had started out in Munster & Leinster's Killarney branch in the 1950s and ended up chairing one of the top-fifty banks in the United States. He had been the embodiment in the Baltimore-Washington area of a great source of pride to Irish people, the Irish ownership of a big and respectable Maryland bank. He had become a pillar of Baltimore civic life as a director of the Rouse Company, Catholic Charities, the Ireland-United States Council for Commerce & Industry and the World Trade Centre Institute in Baltimore. He was also a trustee of Mercy Health Services and The Walters Art Gallery, where he had once sponsored a big exhibition of Irish art.

Casey, Tom Mulcahy and four other directors of the sixteen-member board stood down when the Allfirst board met on 30 April and a new twelve-member board was elected. It included two new

members, Eugene Sheehy and Michael Sullivan, former US ambassador to Ireland and also a member of the AIB board.

The Allfirst board also re-elected Michael Buckley as a director.
Much had been made of the fact that Buckley was chief executive of
AIB for only eight months when the fraud was uncovered, but he
had also been on the board of Allfirst since 27 April 1999, the same
day Susan Keating became a director.

Buckley had taken a lot of heat over his handling of the tip from
a market source in May 2001 of heavy foreign exchange trading at
Allfirst. He had called David Cronin to discuss the matter and was
satisfied by Cronin's reply and thought no more of it. 'It simply left my
mind,' he had said. AIB's relationship with Cronin was, however,
problematical. As Dublin's man in Baltimore, he had been protected
as the best person for the job when questions about his performance
were raised by Bramble and Keating, but senior officers of AIB 'also
recognised that the Allfirst treasurer's level of energy and commitment were lower than expected,' and Buckley had told Ludwig that
he was 'prepared ultimately to change the Allfirst's treasurer's reporting line or remove him if the existing arrangements did not work out.'

The 'existing arrangements' were that Cronin reported directly to
Susan Keating at Allfirst. After she became chief executive, Keating
wanted Cronin to report to a new chief financial officer to 'more
closely monitor his activities.' At the time Mulcahy was AIB group
chief executive. AIB insisted the reporting arrangement should stand,
as it was important for Keating to understand treasury operations and
this was 'best accomplished' by having Cronin report directly to her.
In effect, Keating told AIB that Cronin should report to someone
else who understood treasury operations better, and AIB told Keating
that Cronin should report to her as she should understand treasury
operations better.

The argument went to the heart of the matter. AIB had so little
control over its American subsidiary that it relied heavily on Cronin
as the most important point of contact, and resisted any hint of
demotion. Keating told Ludwig that she went along with the
arrangement because 'she perceived that AIB would be displeased if
the treasurer's reporting line were changed.'

Buckley said he had not told Bramble or Keating about his
contact with Cronin, as 'nobody ever expressed any concerns about

David Cronin's competence. The issues had more to do with management style rather than competence as a treasury manager.'

In future, recommended Ludwig, 'the chairmen and chief executives of AIB and of any AIB operating units at which any trading
operations are conducted should affirmatively take full responsibility
for the trading activities of the bank – these activities are risky and
should not be undertaken unless they are "part of the mainstream" of
the bank.'

Intriguingly, an AIB audit team was in Allfirst just before the
crisis broke. Rusnak thought they were checking him out. An AIB
spokesperson said, 'They were there to discuss general auditing procedures. It was a sheer coincidence they were there just before the
fraud was discovered.'

Buckley actually met Rusnak just over three months after the
market alert in May 2001. In September, a few days before the
terrorist attacks on the United States, the AIB group chief executive
visited Baltimore as part of a tour of AIB's overseas outposts. Rusnak
told a friend that, to his surprise, he was invited to join a group of
executives assembled to greet Buckley. The head of the bank and the
trader exchanged a few polite words. They did not discuss business.

The aftermath of the Rusnak losses was a very difficult period for
Buckley. He had to forfeit his first year's bonus as chief executive,
which could have been worth up to €250,000. His plans for AIB were
thrown awry. He had once pledged that the Baltimore bank would be
a long-term investment and an integral part of its operations. Now
he had had to fight for his own survival because Allfirst had screwed
everything up.

It would, however, have been difficult for the AIB board to
accept his offer to stand down. AIB would have become vulnerable
to a takeover. The bank might have appeared rudderless, making it
more likely that Lochlann Quinn would receive at least a tentative
approach from another bank in Ireland or the UK interested in a
takeover. And there was no obvious replacement. AIB's head of
finance and risk, Gary Kennedy, had been a strong contender. But he
had joined AIB only five years previously and he too was damaged by
the affair. He had been a board member of Allfirst since April 1998,
and was the AIB executive responsible for overseeing the group's risk
functions for most of the five-year period during which the fraud

occurred. Eugene Sheehy lacked experience in managing the bank's international businesses but most insiders saw him as odds-on favourite to succeed Buckley sometime in the future.

David Cronin was singled out for culpability by AIB after the Ludwig report was published on 14 March. Buckley said he felt 'absolutely betrayed by somebody in a position in whom the bank had a lot of trust.' AIB chairman, Lochlann Quinn told RTÉ listeners, his voice angry, that no one questioned Cronin's abilities but Cronin 'wasn't working hard enough' and had an 'attitude' problem and Rusnak had been able to carry out his fraud only because Cronin and Ray failed in their jobs.

Cronin did come out badly from the whole affair, especially in his handling of the market tip to Buckley. Before sending a reply to Buckley's query about the level of foreign exchange trading, he got his secretary to e-mail a draft copy to Rusnak, which the trader called up on his laptop. Rusnak told a friend later that it contained net rather than gross figures, and that even then the figures were much too low. At a press conference in Dublin on 14 April, Ludwig's associate, Duncan Hennas, said: 'Mr Cronin's e-mail back to Mr Buckley was, as I said, categorical; it was also wrong, in fact the volumes were higher than he reported.' He added, 'It's hard to explain why Mr Cronin didn't take this inquiry more seriously.'

Eugene Ludwig nevertheless took a liking to David Cronin and did not question his integrity. 'I actually feel badly for David Cronin,' he said. 'We interviewed him for eight, ten hours and I thought he was credible and I honestly thought he was a decent fellow. Facts may prove otherwise. I don't think so.' 'I think Rusnak fooled him,' he said. 'I think he was sort of like a bloodhound. I think Rusnak hurt his sniffer a bit by being devious.'

His words echoed something Rusnak said to a friend after it was all over, that he believed someone knew from late-2001 that the auditors were on the way and that the groundwork was laid from that time to make the case that Rusnak was 'the evil genius that fooled us.'

As David Cronin escaped the heat of the inquisition for the dusty heat of Egypt, where he took his wife, Karen, for a holiday, residents of Ruxton Riderwood expressed anger over what they saw as the scapegoating of a popular neighbour who was an active citizen, involved in the Catholic Church, and a board member of the

Baltimore chapter of the Boy Scouts of America and Catholic Charities. His lawyer, Michael Colglazier, said 'the bank has done a great disservice to a highly-principled man whose business acumen and sense of integrity and loyalty has served the bank's interests for many years,' and concerns over 'the overriding political and institutional objectives influencing the outcome of the investigation were warranted.'

Stella O'Leary, a prominent Irishwoman living in Washington and a fellow-graduate of University College Dublin, said Cronin was universally loved and admired in the Irish community for his warmth and generosity. 'His social gatherings are, as we Irish remember at home: family, song, story and good *craic*. He didn't have any of the pretensions often associated with corporate executives.'

Bob Ray and his wife, Kojii, were furious at the way Cronin had been treated. 'Our family, as well as others who have been affected by this tragedy, are appalled at how John Rusnak has been immortalised and David Cronin has been crucified in the Irish press and by others,' Kojii Ray told journalist Paul Teetley.

John Rusnak was not among the fifty-five staff members and former employees of AIB and Allfirst interviewed by Ludwig and his team. That was 'normal' said Ludwig, as the trader was being investigated by the FBI. He formed the conclusion, however, that Rusnak was an 'incredibly devious' trader who had taken in both Cronin and Ray. 'He was very clever, he was a good talker,' he said. 'The fraud was carefully planned and meticulously executed.'

As for Bob Ray, he was 'a very arrogant individual,' who 'inexplicably ignored numerous warning signs of Mr Rusnak's activity,' said the former US Comptroller of the Currency. 'He was very proud of his own prowess in trading interest rates... If someone would question him he was pretty strong in terms of his views.' A colleague of Ray's from earlier days remembered him, however, as 'one of the most compassionate people in the bank when you got to know him.'

Ludwig and his team also did not interview AIB's and Allfirst's auditors PricewaterhouseCoopers, which failed to detect the fraud over five years. Lochlann Quinn initially appeared to absolve PwC of any accountability over the Allfirst foreign exchange fraud. He said it was 'not the job of auditors to disclose fraud.' The fundamental responsibility rested with Allfirst management and systems. In April, however, AIB pointedly dropped PwC as its group auditors, replacing it with the accountancy firm KPMG. Despite AIB's 'highest regard' for PwC, the audit firm was not invited to participate in the tender. PwC retained consulting work for the bank in the information technology and taxation areas. According to the AIB annual report the bank paid €1.8 million for the 2001 audit and another €900,000 for related services. However, the information technology consultancy was worth €400,000, taxation services another €600,000 and other consultancy €1.2 million. Some 73 percent of the total audit services fees were paid to overseas offices of the auditors in the US, the UK and Poland.

PwC's relationship with AIB had come in for sharp public criticism in December 1999 when a sub-committee of the Dáil's Public Accounts Committee found that AIB and its auditors had failed to make provision in the audited accounts of the bank for massive potential DIRT liabilities that could have impinged on the bank's solvency.

When AIB shareholders met in June to approve the appointment of KPMG to act as auditors, deputy chairman, John McGuckian, suggested that the bank had 'made no decision on PwC' regarding further action. Buckley, however, repeated to the *Irish Times* that the bank had always taken the view that what had happened at Allfirst was due to management failure. 'How many more lashes do you want us to give ourselves?' he asked wearily.

By an extraordinary coincidence, in the same week at the end of April that AIB announced that it was dumping PwC, the audit firm was fined £250,000 in London and £635,000 costs by a British government accountancy watchdog for its failure to spot the gaping financial hole created by Nick Leeson at Barings Bank seven years earlier. The UK Joint Disciplinary Tribunal listed a series of failures of Coopers & Lybrand, now part of PwC. The audit firm had already paid an estimated £70 million in a High Court settlement after a case for negligence in its Barings audit was taken by KPMG, liquidators to Barings after its spectacular collapse in 1995. The liquidators claimed that forgery and a range of other methods were used to cover the losses and that the audited accounts were false. Another action seeking $200 million compensation was continuing in the London High Court against Deloitte & Touche, the firm that audited the accounts of Barings' ill-fated Singapore subsidiary in 1992 and 1993.

The progress of this case was being watched closely by Nick Leeson. Once it was over, his financial arrangements with the liquidators would be reviewed. So as not to profit overtly from wrong-doing, the 'rogue trader' had to pay the liquidators 50 per cent of his earnings from speaking engagements and risk management conferences. This was a lot of money. Soon after his release from jail in 1999 for example, he was paid £60,000 to speak on the state of the world's financial markets to the Dutch Stock Exchange, each member of which paid £200 to listen to his views. During his talks Leeson took some credit for new controls that had been put in place in international trading markets.

'When I speak to traders now, they tell me about how much more difficult it is to make money because of the controls put in place after Barings. Not many of them thank me for it,' Leeson told a risk management conference at the Business Forums International in London in May 2001. 'The chances of this happening again are absolutely zero,' he added.

Legal action against auditors had been taken successfully by AIB before. The bank sued the accounting firm Ernst & Whinney, now part of Ernst & Young, which had advised AIB on the value of the Insurance Corporation of Ireland before AIB purchased it in 1983. In a High Court action against Ernst & Whinney, AIB claimed that it had been misled about the real financial position of the collapsed insurer. AIB secured £38.5 million in compensation.

Another casualty of the Rusnak affair was AIB's head of group internal audit, 43-year-old Eugene McErlean, even though he had no authority to audit, or responsibility for, Allfirst, a problem that went to the heart of the whole affair. After launching the Ludwig report, AIB issued a statement dated 14 March detailing 'actions to address issues raised by fraudulent trading activities.' In a list of specific measures it said: 'The position of Head of Group Internal Audit falls due to be filled in the normal way later this year. This position will be filled by an external appointment.' McErlean complained that this was a disciplinary sanction taken without any complaint or charge and was in breach of internal procedures. The bank wanted to 'scapegoat him for the debacle at Allfirst,' he said. McErlean issued High Court proceedings to retain his position as internal auditor and for damages for defamation, stigma, conspiracy, intimidation and breach of contract. The bank said that McErlean's term of office was due to end and that he had not been dismissed. The internal audit function did not have any remit over Allfirst. McErlean's proceedings are ongoing.

In his report, Ludwig highlighted the critical failure in AIB's management of its subsidiary, saying, 'There should be a clear understanding that the responsibility for having a robust internal audit function at all business units ultimately rests with the head of AIB group audit.' Its sufficiency should be 'carefully monitored' by the AIB audit committee.

In a statement AIB said, 'The position of Chief Risk Officer will be filled by an external appointee in the near future. In this connection the retirement of Mr Pat Ryan, AIB Group Treasurer, which was announced on 8 January, will take effect from 2 June 2002.' AIB also announced that 'an individual of international standing' would be appointed to review and advise the AIB board on risk management organisation across the group. It chose John G Heimann, also a former Comptroller of the Currency in the United States, and one-time chairman of Merrill Lynch Global Financial Institutions, who was subsequently appointed to the AIB board as a group special risk management adviser on the issues raised by Ludwig. First Manhattan, one of the world's leading financial consultancy groups, was also hired to work with AIB's capital markets division. The costs of the Rusnak affair kept going up.

The speed with which Allied Irish Banks recapitalised its US subsidiary and the steps it took to address the causes of the debacle enabled the bank to avoid severe punitive action by US regulators.

The Federal Reserve Board in Washington – the United States' central bank – had a scale of responses to banking scandals: the first and least serious entailed a private letter, the second entailed a signed agreement not made public, and the third entailed a written agreement made public. Where a bank failed to take action and was uncooperative, and in more serious cases where bank clients suffered losses, the feds could impose a heavy monetary fine and issue a cease-and-desist order to stop trading. It could also issue a prohibition notice on individuals against working in a registered banking institution.

After a three-month joint investigation the US Federal Reserve decided on the third option. It required AIB and Allfirst to sign a

written, public agreement on the further steps it was taking to remedy
the weaknesses at Allfirst. The agreement set out the measures to be
adopted by AIB and a timetable for informing the regulators of
action taken on the basis of the Ludwig report and other reviews by
outside consultants. It was published on 16 May by the Federal
Reserve Board in Washington and signed by Jeffrey Kane of the
Federal Reserve Bank of Richmond, Mary Louise Preis, Maryland
commissioner of financial regulation, Adrian Byrne of the Central
Bank of Ireland, Michael Buckley, group chief executive of AIB, and
Susan Keating, chief executive of Allfirst.

It included a requirement that within one-hundred-and-eighty
days, the boards of AIB and Allfirst should make available for super-
visory review written details of any management and operational
changes made as a result of the banks' review of risk management
procedures. The embarrassment of this public calling to account was
offset by the acknowledgement that 'the bank properly recognised
the need to take appropriate actions to improve management oversight, day to day risk management, internal controls, audit standards,
management information systems and policies and procedures for
treasury management and operations functions.'

On top of all this, AIB faced legal actions from investors. In the
United States, class action suits were initiated against the bank by a
Washington law firm, Finkelstein, Thompson & Loughran, along
with two New York-based firms, Stull, Stull & Brody and Bernstein
Liebhard & Lifshitz. They represented investors who acquired AIB
American Depositary Receipts (ADRs) between 6 February 1999
and 6 February 2002, during which time the bank's financial
statements failed through fraud to reflect the $691 million currency
losses, and sought as much as $50 million. The Ludwig report left a
lot of questions unanswered, said Conor Crowley, an attorney for
Finkelstein, Thompson & Loughran.

One of those questions was where the missing money went to.

From the start, AIB played down the likelihood of being able to
recover any of the $691 million. The money had been swallowed up
by other banks with which Rusnak made bad or unhedged bets.
However, it hired Kroll, the US security and investigation company,
to follow the money trail and to discover whether the trader colluded
with anybody else.

If involvement in the fraud by counterparties at other banks were confirmed, it could support AIB's claims of a complex conspiracy and not just a collapse of internal controls. Most banks insured against losses arising from fraud or theft by employees through a fidelity policy and AIB was said by market sources to have self-insured against some risk through its own offshore insurance company. AIB declined to disclose its insurance arrangements to the media. Most investors had written-off any prospect of a successful insurance claim. John Kelly of NCB Stockbrokers said, 'They would be silly not to try and get some money back, but I don't think anybody is counting on it.'

The bank's investigators did not examine the activities of third parties involved in Rusnak's massive trading. Rusnak's activities 'may also have been facilitated by individuals at other firms,' said Ludwig, but they 'did not have an opportunity to talk to the foreign currency traders with whom Mr Rusnak dealt.' Many people in the foreign exchange business had asked why traders were not more suspicious of what Rusnak was doing, especially when he took out the five huge synthetic loans amounting to $300 million in 2001. Rusnak himself felt that the other banks knew he was vulnerable and took advantage of his desperation.

The banks with which Rusnak did the deep-in-the-money deals during 2001 conducted their own internal inquiries. They refused to make the results public. However, two foreign exchange salesmen from Citibank, which loaned Rusnak $125 million in February 2001, were fired six weeks after the discovery of Rusnak's losses at Allfirst. Citibank said that the two were dismissed 'for reasons unrelated to trading activity,' reported to be improper entertainment, and it had found 'no evidence that any of our employees colluded with Mr Rusnak or anyone else at Allfirst.' One of them was Richard Marra, whose name was on a slip of paper kept behind the bar in Peter's Pour House in Baltimore, to be used to pick up the tab for Rusnak and his friends. The other was Joseph Craven, who worked for Citibank in Singapore. Bank of America, which loaned Rusnak $75 million in March, said it had reviewed its dealings with the Baltimore bank and found 'no evidence that any Bank of America employee colluded' with him.

Because of the unusual nature of some of Rusnak's trades, other banks should have asked questions about their dealings with him,

Ludwig said. 'The size and scope of Mr Rusnak's trading activities would certainly have appeared unusual to anyone paying attention at the counterparty firms,' but to date 'we have only a limited record of the prime brokers communicating or attempting to communicate with personnel at Allfirst at a level above Mr Rusnak.' He recommended to AIB that 'unusual trades should be fully reviewed to ensure that no impropriety took place and to clarify fully whether the prime brokers or other dealers or personnel at these firms obtained any benefits in their dealings with Mr Rusnak other than full bid-offer spreads and market fees.'

The proprietary trading desk at Allfirst was permanently closed down by AIB after the fraud was uncovered. 'Trading by lone wolves should be highly discouraged,' said Ludwig. 'Trading activity performed in a team environment is more likely to be controlled.'

The Federal Reserve was deeply unhappy with what had happened in Baltimore. In a pointed warning to other banks, a US Federal Reserve Bank panel reissued copies of its 'Guidelines for Foreign Exchange Activity' to the chief executives of all financial houses with currency trading desks. US Federal Reserve Governor, Susan Schmidt Bies, ticked off AIB in a speech in Virginia. Banks must maintain controls for their foreign affiliates, she said, citing the problems at Allied Irish Banks. 'History has shown that foreign affiliates are particularly vulnerable to internal control problems. In most cases these losses could have been avoided by ensuring the bank's control procedures – for example, segregation of duties and the conduct of thorough and independent internal audits – were functioning properly.'

At the AIB shareholders' meeting in Belfast on 29 May, Lochlann Quinn apologised for the lapses that allowed the fraud to occur. 'Like everyone else in this room I was shocked when I first heard about the scale of the loss,' he said. 'Since the fraud came to light the board has taken steps to ensure that such an event can never happen again. What happened was devastating and shouldn't have happened.' With AIB shares trading at around €15, about 9 per cent above their pre-scandal level, the shareholders were, with some noisy exceptions, suitably mollified.

Quinn and Buckley dismissed newspaper speculation of a merger with Bank of Ireland, an unlikely eventuality in any event in the light of a decision by the EU Commission in 2001 to block proposals for a Swedish merger between SEB and Swedbank involving a smaller combined market share than the two leading Irish banks, which had almost 65 per cent of deposits between them. The speculation was revived, however, when AIB and Bank of Ireland reached agreement to share their information technology systems to allow them to process transactions more cheaply, although this idea was later abandoned.

In the wake of the scandal there was a widespread assumption in Maryland that the Irish would pull out of Baltimore. Things looked bleak. The damage was most evident in the early days, when Allfirst lost some $10 million in deposits, despite assurances that AIB would meet the losses. The bank received a reduced credit rating from Standard & Poor's after the scandal, a measure that normally increased the cost of any wholesale borrowing by the bank from a Federal Reserve bank member. In the first half of 2002 profits fell by 25 per cent. Market research showed a drop in customer satisfaction over the losses. By the end of March 2002 the scandal had cost the bank another $14.3 million as it attempted to repair the damage. Some $8.3 million was paid to Eugene Ludwig and his team of investigators, and to lawyers and consultants who examined its risk management processes. Another $6 million was spent on advertising and public relations consultants to restore confidence amongst its customers.

AIB had not, after all, played that well in the 'biggest game in town.' On the day Bramble took over, NationsBank, two-hundred miles to the south, was much the same size; today it is enormous,' said a former First Maryland executive vice-president.

'Allfirst really has not been a player to speak of as far as acquisitions go in the mid-Atlantic relevant to others out there,' said Adam Barkstrom, a banking analyst for Legg Mason. 'Although AIB has previously discussed expanding its operations in the US, we wouldn't be at all surprised to see these assets go up for sale once the brouhaha dies down,' said Kathy Shanley, at GimmeCredit of New York. 'It is absolutely my opinion that AIB will sell Allfirst,' said Lew Sosnowik, a bank analyst with Koonce Securities in Bethesda, Maryland. 'They never expanded the venture to become a real powerhouse in the United States, and now that it has turned out to be a disaster, my guess is that they will try to "gussy" it up a bit and get rid of it. Excluding the trading problems, Allfirst is a good bank and would have many interested buyers – particularly banks in the Midwest or the Northeast.'

Even if it was their intention, Quinn and Buckley could not put up a 'for sale' notice at 25 South Charles Street until the time was right. Buckley talked of turning the bank around, 'getting it right'. Quinn said, 'We have one of the largest investments by any European bank and it's a position we are convinced we are going to make work.' However, Gary Kennedy, AIB Group's financial director, indicated that the great goal of acquisitions that had driven Paddy O'Keefe, Gerry Scanlan, Tom Mulcahy and Jerry Casey back in the 1980s had not been achieved. He said after the annual general meeting that AIB had suspended plans to acquire other banks in the mid-Atlantic region. They must determine first whether the Allfirst name had been eroded by the scandal. 'If you have a sore tooth you take it out, but the pain doesn't go away right away,' he told Andrew Ratner of the *Baltimore Sun*. 'You have to see if there's infection underneath.'

Many of AIB's major shareholders saw the Baltimore bank itself as the sore tooth that should be removed. They said they believed it was time for the Irish bank to get rid of its US subsidiary. A number of fund managers told the *Irish Times* that they were broadly satisfied with AIB's handling of the $691 million fraud but wanted to see the bank exit the US market. Joe O'Dwyer, fund manager at Montgomery Oppenheim, said many of the institutions had sent very strong messages to the bank about its Baltimore investment. 'AIB has been told we do not expect to see it put any new capital into Allfirst,' he said. 'The goodwill attached to it has been damaged and the value of that franchise has fallen. We would want to see signs of it being rebuilt within a year.'

It was a far cry from the 'secret love affair' of 1983 when AIB put the ring on First Maryland's finger and both sides had high hopes of creating a perfect transatlantic alliance. For a decade, AIB's approach seemed a model for foreign businesses and financial institutions seeking to acquire a subsidiary in the United States. 'Think about it,' said an AIB veteran. 'A company from a little nation had the balls to have a go at being serious in US banking. It was a hell of a disappointment that AIB had to take this trading shit.' But the union was flawed because of profound and underestimated cultural differences, personality clashes and fundamental disagreements about what banking was about. 'It is a story of tremendous original vision, poor execution, ultimate neglect, and dreadful price paid,' said the AIB source.

AIB's highly-praised strategy of running its subsidiary with a 'light hand' became seriously undermined once it decided it wanted much more than the annual revenue derived from the conservative banking policies of the management it inherited. In the process AIB effectively ceded control of the operations of its subsidiary. The board in Allfirst was, in theory, subject to AIB's one hundred per cent shareholding, but most of its members were selected by the chairman in Baltimore and were sympathetic to his position. A feeling that they had little say in the bank's internal affairs and controls may explain why the small number of AIB directors missed so many board meetings in Baltimore.

The bank's filings to the Securities and Exchange Commission showed that during 1999 and 2000 Michael Buckley did not attend 75 per cent of the aggregate of the meetings of the Allfirst board of directors and of board committees on which he served. Gary Kennedy, AIB Group financial director, did not attend at least 75 per cent of such meetings during 2000 and 2001, and Tom Mulcahy did not attend 75 per cent of such meetings during 2000. The 'light hand' approach meant that AIB's only real contact with the bank in the crucial years of Rusnak's fraud was David Cronin, the 'home office spy'.

Ludwig called Allfirst 'a typical American old-style commercial bank, that typically engaged in taking deposits and making loans.' Yet it was owned by an international bank which had foreign currency trading activity as part of its financial activity overseas, and this encouraged AIB's point man in Baltimore to get in on the act by hiring Rusnak.

It didn't work. As an analyst at a major Wall Street firm put it: 'The odds against someone in Allfirst being able to beat the market consistently, without being a top-rated hedge fund with state-of-the-art execution ability and fundamental technical research, are enormous. Markets have become highly efficient with little opportunity to make money from directional bets. Anyone who thought otherwise didn't realise that the good old days were over and were hoping that the "time-travel" magic would continue.'

Eventually this led to the ludicrous situation where, removed from the controls AIB exercised over its other treasury operations, the 'lone-wolf' trader would move markets worldwide, where he would become known as a big-time player in Nick Leeson's old haunts in Singapore, where he would be given holiday trips by the big New York banks as they fell over themselves for his business, where a major New York bank would call AIB to ask if it was good for a billion dollars to cover a settlement in a 'typical American old-style commercial bank'.

And nobody did anything about it until it was too late.

18

Postscript

While Ludwig had been investigating the fraud for the bank, United States Attorney Thomas M DiBiagio was compiling a case against Rusnak in what he described as the 'largest bank fraud in the US in the past decade.'

From the start it was evident that the FBI and the US Justice Department did not believe the trader had been stealing the money. He was allowed to live at home, though he had surrendered his passport. He moved around freely while giving weekly interviews to the FBI officials on his case. Everything he told them checked out with the Ludwig report which described his trading tricks and deceptions in great detail. Like Ludwig, DiBiagio said the investigation into the bank's losses was still continuing. He declined to comment on the possibility of charges against other persons who might have helped Rusnak. 'That would jeopardise the ongoing investigation,' he said.

On 5 June DiBiagio brought Rusnak before a Special Federal Grand Jury in Baltimore. The trader was indicted on seven counts of bank fraud and false entry into bank records related to the losses of $691 million at Allfirst. The indictment did not allege that Rusnak received any of the funds that made up the $691 million loss but that he received salary and bonuses amounting to more than $850,000 from 1997 through 2001, not including the $220,000 bonus that Allfirst did not pay him after it discovered the loss. Each count of the indictment carried a maximum penalty of thirty years imprisonment, a $1 million fine and up to five years of supervised release after serving a term of imprisonment. Specifically he was charged with submitting to bank officials documents (evidently the ones he printed out from his 'Fake Docs' file) fraudulently confirming fictitious foreign currency options, and entering fictitious foreign currency option trades into the bank's Devon system with Citibank, Bank of America, Deutsche Bank, Merrill Lynch and Bank of New York.

Rusnak then appeared before United States Magistrate Judge Beth P Gesner in the federal court ten minutes walk from Allfirst headquarters in Baltimore. He was released without bail pending formal arraignment. His lawyer, David Irwin, and Pastor Joe Ehrmann were by his side for the five-minute appearance. His client, said Irwin, 'continues to be truly remorseful for his role in these events and we look forward to the eventual resolution of this.' In Dublin, AIB issued a statement after Rusnak was charged saying that from the outset it believed 'it was the victim of a complex and sophisticated fraud and these charges endorse that conclusion.'

While the Ludwig report identified Rusnak as the 'lone wolf' responsible for the fraud, its account of how the trader's superiors protected him at critical moments pointed to a possible line of defence. In 1994 Joseph Jett, the 36-year-old head of Kidder Peabody's bond trading desk, was fired for losing the firm $350 million. (Where Michael Buckley said the news of Rusnak's losses hit him like a bereavement, the first reaction of Jack Welch, chairman of General Electric which owned Kidder Peabody, was, he said, to throw up.) Jett, who had been Kidder's 'man of the year' and received a $9 million bonus for his supposed trading success, was cleared of fraud on the grounds that people above him knew what he was doing. Those above Rusnak did not know of his fraud but did know about his extraordinarily heavy trading.

Whatever the outcome, Rusnak joined a unique gallery of rogue traders. Top of the list was Yasuo Hamanaka, jailed for eight years after losing $2.6 billion trading copper for Japan's Sumitomo company in 1996. Then came Nick Leeson, jailed for six years in 1995 for losing £850 million and bringing down Barings Bank. Toshihide Iguchi was jailed for four years for losing $1.1 billion in unauthorised bond trades while with Daiwa Bank in 1995. Another trader, Peter Young of Deutsche Morgan Grenfell, lost £400 million at its UK management arm after breaking investment rules. He had a mental breakdown and tried to castrate himself and he later appeared in court dressed as a woman.

Rusnak had changed in appearance since the day he left the bank. Then he was drawn and haggard-looking. He had been burning up nervous energy at a furious pace for months. Within a few weeks he had added ten pounds, and at his court appearance it was evident he had put on quite a few more.

On 11 June 2002 Rusnak was summoned before US Magistrate Judge Paul Grimm in a Baltimore court to be formally arraigned. 'We are pleading not guilty to all counts,' said Irwin. The hearing lasted five minutes. The trial date was set for 10 February 2003 and two weeks allotted for the trial. Rusnak was free again, without bail, to await the trial or the outcome of a possible plea bargain between his lawyer and the US Attorney. Under US federal practice, a plea bargain could be negotiated whereby Rusnak would change his plea to guilty in the anticipation of receiving a lesser sentence by saving the government the necessity of a trial.

After the brief hearing, Rusnak told court personnel: 'Someday no one will care about me anymore. I'm looking forward to that day.'

Index